MW00617226

ALL *my* BEST

WISDOM AND ENCOURAGEMENT FOR A BETTER LIFE

Carlos,
Thanks for Being
The Leader You
Are. I Am/proud
To Be Your Friend,
All my Best
Tommy Newberry

Edited by Jacqui Scherrer, Poison Pen Proofreading

Cover design by David Kennedy of Lewis Creative Media
www.lewiscrtv.com

Learn more about the author at
amazon.com/author/terryweaver

or

www.terryweaverbooks.com

Connect with Terry on Facebook
www.facebook.com/terryweaverbooks/

ISBN
978-1-7330902-4-7 (paperback)
978-1-7330902-5-4 (electronic book)

This one is for you

CHELLEY

the love of my life.

Table of Contents

INTRODUCTION 1

A DREAM 3

FEAR 6

HOPE 12

CRITICISM 15

CHALLENGES 22

WORK 26

THE HERD 30

DESPERATION 34

GENIUS 38

ANGER 44

WORDS 48

FORGIVENESS 52

GOOD AND EVIL 54

GARDENING 58

LOVE 61

SEEKING 65

PERFECTION 68

MENTAL MAPS 72

WORSHIP 77

IDENTITY 81

THE MIND 86

STRATEGY 90

FUNDAMENTALISM 94

INFLUENCE 101

MORE 107

BUSYNESS 110

FOCUS 113

CONNECTION 118

TIME TRAVEL 122

COMPANY 125

COMMUNICATION 129

SUPERPOWER 132

WISDOM 134

RESPONSIBILITY 138

SERVICE 143

CREATIVITY 147

ADVENTURE 153

CONCLUSION 156

QUOTE INDEX 157

REFERENCES 169

ABOUT THE AUTHOR 174

Introduction

Sometimes, when looking at the world we live in, I am saddened and left with a choice to make about the inequities that surround me. The choice lies deep in my soul and demands an answer. The question may not be asked of everyone, but it's a question that I am compelled by responsibility to answer; that question is, 'Will you turn a blind eye and accept the way things are, or will you use whatever resources, internal and external, however small or large, to affect change in the world?'

This small book is my best attempt to affect change. It is a message to those who are looking for ways to improve their lives. In it, I have chosen three dozen or so topics that I believe are very important to all of us who wrestle through the uncertainty of life.

The book is written to give you tools and ideas to consider, to help you navigate your journey of becoming. It is meant to be used as a companion guide, something that can be referred back to often. My hope is that these carefully selected words can travel with you and provide a little strength and hope when you are frustrated, weary, or just need a few words of encouragement.

These writings are *All my Best.* They come from four decades of living, but also from the giants—mentors, friends, leaders, teachers, and authors—I have had the privilege to learn from and walk among. They carry lessons from war, brokenness, addiction, heartbreak, and the many other trials and triumphs common among us all.

My greatest desire is that something in this book will give you strength today, for today is all we really have.

A Dream

"The tragedy of life is what dies
inside a man while he lives."
Albert Schweitzer

Do you have a dream? I am referring to a dream that fills and enlivens your waking hours, not the dream we sometimes experience in a deep slumber. A vital component to a fulfilled life is having a dream, something we look forward to. Dreams invigorate us, help stir up our passion, and give us fuel to move through life with purpose.

When we have a dream to chase, our days are filled with motion, energy that helps propel us forward toward a prize. The human mind has the ability to construct new ideas for the future, to dream of alternate realities, to paint a picture of a better tomorrow, but many of us fail to dream. Many have abdicated one of their most powerful abilities, the ability to dream.

Hope is the substance that fuels our dreams; it is essential to life. Without hope, the future dims and our journey through life becomes merely a belabored walk, in place of an epic adventure. When we have something to look forward to, a dream to chase down, our lives become impregnated with meaning. When someone is inspired by a dream, everything changes, there is a cadence to their movement. Each day becomes a point on a map that leads to a great destination.

When we discover a dream born from hope, our days weave together to create a passion-filled journey. But without a dream, life becomes something less meaningful, a march of indifference, something plain, void of emotion. Without the passion of a dream to charge our days, life feels more like a trudge toward mediocrity, an existence without the thrill of endless possibility.

Earl Nightingale was one of fifteen surviving Marines on the USS Arizona, one of the ships attacked on December 7th, 1941, at Pearl Harbor. His experience taught him a lesson about the fragility of life. Nightingale went on to inspire millions of lives before passing in 1989; his words meet us today: "Never give up on a dream just because of the time it will take to accomplish it. The time will pass anyway."

Dr. Albert Schweitzer explained the vital importance of having a dream when he said, "The tragedy of life is what dies inside a man while he lives." When we fail to chase our dreams, something deep down inside of us dies, day by day.

If you are reading this and realizing you lack a dream, it is never too late to start dreaming again; begin today. Oftentimes, dreams are somewhere inside of us, only needing to be unearthed. Dreams are often covered in fear, lying dormant, but they are still there awaiting a resurrection. If this sounds morbid, that's because it is— to kill a dream is the same as snuffing a piece of our life, a heinous self-crime. Unfortunately, many teachers, coaches, and parents are dream killers whether they know it or not. But dreams can be brought back to life; to do so, one must autopsy their hope and do everything within their power to regain it, for hope is the voice of our dreams, and however faint the voice, it calls us to better things.

Without a dream, one cannot be fulfilled—we need something to strive for, to reach toward, because to chase a dream is vital to happiness. It leads to a life bursting with vigor and purpose. Without a dream, our lives are hindered—thrown out of rhythm, and we are left longing for vitality. A dream can wake us from our sleepy existence. Do you have a dream?

Fear

*"The price of our vitality is the sum
of all our fears." David Whyte*

Fear is our greatest enemy. It has a way of paralyzing our future. Our minds seem to cling to fear and be wired for preservation by way of risk aversion. Many claim that our fear is rooted in our prehistoric evolution; whether it is or not, we should question fear, inspect it for what it truly is, and look at unhealthy fear as our enemy.

Our fears are much more numerous than our actual dangers. Think about the preceding statement for a minute, and ask if it is true. For me, the statement is true. When was the last time you were in serious or even grave danger? For most, the answer is never. For me, I have only been in grave danger a handful of times in my lifetime, but still, fear has a way of trying to buckle us to a version of life that is riddled with danger. It's not until we begin to push back against our fears and categorize them accurately, that we are able to experience freedom.

Fear is much different than danger, and because of this, we should do our best to look at fear as objectively as possible and view it as something foreign. Fear's main objective is to box us into a corner and keep us from living free: its greatest measure of success is keeping us from attaining our desires in life. Think back to when you were young—wild at heart and full of imagination. Did you dream of being someone great? Did you dream of being larger than life? As life progressed, what happened to those dreams? Most likely, fear crept in through a backdoor and found a way to kill your dreams, snuffing them out, starving them of life. As we age, societal pressures set in, expectations from ourselves and others begin to mold us, and fear begins to place a stranglehold on our dreams and ambitions.

Fear can be understood as a state of chemical and emotional reaction in response to external or internal stimuli, better known as a threat. It is possible the stimuli are real threats, but most often, these fear producing stimuli are nonthreatening, things like loud noises, prime-time news segments, and most things in the dark. These stimuli produce stress in the brain, and the end result is a biological state of fear. But here's the crux of the matter—both real *and* perceived threats cause fear.

Let me explain with a common fear my family members face, arachnophobia. My wife and kids hate spiders. Every time one is spotted in my house, it creates a real fear, and they call me to extinguish the fear-inducing eight-legged critter. Just the other day, I rushed downstairs because my family was yelling, 'Tarantula!' I arrived at the scene and met my family's threatening enemy, a furry brown half-dollar-sized violin spider. It was positioned next to the wall, close to the back of the couch. My son handed me my weapon, a sandal, and I went to work whacking it, until finally it resembled a creamy brown substance more than it did a spider.

A very similar experience happened just a few weeks prior when my wife was doing some yard work; she discovered a copperhead snake in our backyard. Her shrill call for help beckoned me to her side. After sizing up the creature, I proceeded to decapitate the venom-toting intruder. Both the spider and the snake were very real threats. One may argue against our actions, but in our minds, they needed to go. The problem with fear, however, is that it has a spreading effect. It can become pandemic if not stopped in its tracks and extinguished.

A few weeks after the snake discovery, my wife explained she did not want to go to the area of the yard the snake was found in because of a lingering fear that one of its legless friends may be there. Similarly, every time I pass the area where I killed the violin spider, I wonder if its thirty cousins are behind the couch planning a counterstrike. These effects fear have are what professionals call a recency and proximity effect. Weeks after a snake sighting, my wife is worried another is lurking, and every time I go near the site where I extinguished the big spider, I wonder if a few more are close by.

When fear goes unchecked, it spreads like a wildfire. A fear of spiders can quickly become a fear of any place a spider could be, then multiply to include any place that is dark and unknown in a home, inside a cabinet, behind the couch, or inside every wall! The lines between real and perceived threats morph and multiply without evidence or rationale. Fear can run rampant in one's life if it is not caught, quarantined, and exposed for what it really is—most of the time—just a perceived threat. Our job then, if we want to live free, is to continually recognize and confront our fears.

The day I confronted fear is so vividly locked into my memory, I can almost recount it perfectly. I was twenty years old and had just landed in Kuwait in preparation to invade Iraq. At the time I was a corpsman in the United States Navy stationed with the Marines. Shortly after our plane landed, we loaded onto a bus and were driven through a big city to our base. While on the drive through the city, I saw men holding automatic weapons and wearing Middle Eastern garb—turbans (hijabs), burqas, and Muslim symbols on their clothing; I immediately thought to myself … 'we are in some serious danger.' I began to associate the people I was seeing with danger--I was experiencing an association fear and a proximity fear.

Up until that point, the only men I had seen dressed similarly, some holding weapons, were terrorists, the ones the news outlets flashed up constantly while covering the 9/11 attacks. A replay of the Twin Towers crashing down in flames replayed in my mind as soon as I saw the Kuwaiti militants, who were in fact, at the time, allies of U.S. military forces. But because of my experience, these men became threats; when I saw them,

I imagined them as bearded men, wearing turbans and hijacking planes, ultimately taking the lives of thousands of innocent people. It did not help that we were heading into a hostile war zone; I was struck with fear, fear of impending doom.

Something else happened that day, and I am not sure why, but I am grateful for it. When I checked into my unit in Kuwait, I remember thinking to myself, 'I will probably die over here,' and for some strange reason, I accepted the possibility. I made a decision to release any false control I had over my life. I made a mental agreement with myself—I was no longer going to fear death, and only then was I able to live with a little freedom. Up until that point I was trying to live and simultaneously control the infinite potential dangers that surrounded me. Fear had me in its clutches, it had a stranglehold on me and was preventing me from living.

Perceived danger can very quickly turn into real fear if we do not take time to analyze the source of the danger and try to understand where the root of the fear is coming from. Only then can we make a decision if the threat is a real or perceived threat we are dealing with. When analyzing and determining if a fear is real or perceived, we can ask ourselves a few questions that will help us confront the reality of our threats.

'Can the fear-producing stimuli be seen, touched, smelled, heard, or recognized by another sense?' If the answer to the question is *no*, there is a high possibility that we are experiencing fear rather than danger.

'Have I incorrectly associated a fear with my current reality?' An example might be associating a fear of tarantulas with dark areas because of a past incident that included both tarantulas and dark areas.

I tell you this story because most of the time what holds us back in life is fear, not danger. If we can make an agreement with ourselves that we will no longer let fear hold us back, we can truly begin to live. Even after we make this agreement, we will still wrestle with fear, but we can win the battle by confronting our fears.

When fear begins to rear its ugly face in my life, I often remind myself of a quote from Anaïs Nin:

> *"Life expands and contracts in proportion to one's courage."*

Hope

"What lies behind us and what lies before us are tiny matters, compared to what lies within us." Ralph Waldo Emerson

Hope is a mysterious thing. At times it hides from us, then it appears—just in time, in time to keep our spirits from sinking into the depths of despair. Sometimes it seems as though hope is so far gone, we can hardly remember how it felt when it danced with our souls. When we think back to times filled by hope, we realize it has since discovered an ability to run from us, fleeing into nothing more than an idea, a past time to reminisce. We begin to question it. What is it, this hope, we only faintly remember?

Hope can be thought of as an expectation of greater things to come in the absence of any such evidence. It wanes and surges, fading then filling the mind like a lucid dream. Like the wind, hope is hard to take hold of; even when it is there, it can't be seen—nor can it be captured, held ransom, or demanded from. And despite its elusive nature, it beckons us to greater ideals of the future. It is this hope that inspires us to march into the unknown.

In the absence of hope, a nagging reminder of the past tugs at us, attempting to keep us chained to yesterday and all its mistakes. If we fail to release the past, the bleakness of today, in all its shades of winter, sets in. We find ourselves in constant tension between what is already done and a small glimmer of promise for tomorrow. We find it hard to exist today, in this gift of the present, without hope. But it is all we have—today that is, this moment in time where we are confronted with reality, ushered in with all of its chaos, challenges, and opportunities.

The chaos of the present offers a host of infinite possibilities; at this moment, we wrestle with urges, needs, desires, and fears ... still, we have a choice—to either pursue the direction from where hope beckons us or to remain in the setting concrete of the past. This choice stifles many; nevertheless, it is a choice we must make. Anne Lamott shares that we should live as if we are dying:

> "To live as if we are dying gives us a chance to experience some real presence. Time is so full for people who are dying in a conscious way ...."[1]

Life without hope becomes merely a nebulous idea, something with a void. It holds even death at its bookend, but to live with hope is something much different. Living with hope is active, bursting with the present despite the past and because of the future. True living must be done now; it must be filled with the present. Living with hope expels inertia. To live, you must ask, 'What greatness lies within me?' Then you must answer courageously.

When we lose hope, we must seek it out ... chase it down, knowing that it is tucked away, buried under a few pains of this world that want to keep us from its power. To live, we must release the past—take hold of the present—while firmly gripping the hope we have found that pulls us forward.

Emerson said, "What lies behind us and what lies before us are tiny matters, compared to what lies within us."

What greatness lies within you? What dream have you ignored that is calling you to stand up and charge toward it? Don't wait. Instead, take a small step in that direction—hope is calling you. Wake up tomorrow and take another small step. It's in these small steps of courage where dreams begin to materialize. Hope is the language of our dreams calling us to something much greater.

Criticism

---

*"You don't always have to chop with
the sword of truth. You can point with
it, too." Anne Lamott*

While finalizing the launch details for my second book,
A Dark Day in Texas, I was thinking about how I could
use the book to do some good. I came up with the idea to
give the book away to a few groups of people: police
officers and their spouses, teachers, veterans, and active-
duty military members. The plan was to give away 8,404
copies of my new book to the select groups. The
significance of the number 8,404 is that it was my rate,
job classification number, in the U.S. Navy.

For the launch of my first book, *The Evolution of a
Leader*, I gave away fifty percent of the profit for the first
ninety days of book sales. I selected ten nonprofits and
sent out ten checks—splitting the money between them.
But for the second launch, I was a little more strapped
for cash, so my goal was to give away the actual books
to the groups I had selected.

A few weeks after completing the giveaway, I noticed a
new review came in for my first book. The reviewer's
listed name, at the time, was 'Anonymous 123.' The
masked reviewer gave my book its first one-star review.

Up until that point, the book had twenty-five five-star reviews and nothing but exceptional feedback. The anonymous reviewer said, "Wasn't very well written … unfortunately I'm unable to give less than 1 star."

Strangely enough, despite the anonymous reviewer's clear dissatisfaction with my first book, the same person purchased and reviewed my second book and gave it a two-star review. I find it very strange that an unsatisfied reader would make multiple purchases from the same author.

I share this with you for one reason: because criticism has a way of devastating us—if we allow it to. When I read the reviews, I was angered, confused, and sad, and here is why: I spent more than a year of my life writing the two books, and I used them to do a lot of good. But despite all of the positive reviews my books received and the good I did with them, I allowed one person's remarks to ruin my day.

I have since come to terms with book reviews; they are subjective, so Anonymous 123 had every right to give the books whatever he or she felt they deserved, and I cannot judge the actual reviews, but I still allowed the negative criticism to knock me off a high point in life, and that was a mistake I hope to help prevent you from making.

Here is what I now know: it does not matter how much good is going on around us or in our life, if we are not careful, we can allow one piece of negativity to crush us. One critic can become a source of resentment, and negativity can keep us from doing future good.

A few months after giving away my new book to almost one thousand readers, I heard from another critic. The message came from someone I had gifted the book to, a person who was in the selected groups I had given to. He said the story was not bad but then proceeded to explain that I "didn't know jack," and he ended the email by calling me an "idiot."

Now that I understand how destructive criticism can be, it helps me handle my words with care. I am reminded of the age-old wisdom. 'If you don't have anything good to say, don't say anything at all.'

After some harsh critics blasted me, I decided it would be helpful to come up with a method for handling critics in the future. So, I developed one. These are three practical ways to wisely combat our reaction to criticism: explore the facts, take responsibility, and survey the arena.

Explore the Facts
In my case, the facts were my first book had twenty-five five-star reviews and one negative review. This should have provided me some consolation when I received the negative review, but anger has a way of clouding out rationality. More times than not, criticism is born out of fear or some manifestation of it, anger or jealousy. If we

can keep this in mind, it will be easier to stay focused on the legitimate and ignore or at least handle criticism a little more adeptly.

Take Responsibility

No matter how fair, unfair, or critical another person acts, we are still responsible for our reactions to their behavior. At the end of the day, we have to come to peace with our behaviors; we do this through responsibility. So in my case—with my critics, I could have sent a message to Anonymous 123 saying, 'Take a hike, and at least leave your real name if you are going to bash someone's hard work,' but it would have benefited neither my critic nor anyone else.

I could have also responded with some carefully crafted rebuttal to the person who called me an idiot after I gave him a gift that took many months of my life to produce, but that would have been futile. Instead, these opponents drove me to learn from them and help others learn from them too. We have to take responsibility for the things under our control, and our reactions to criticism are under our control.

Great lessons from past leaders confirm this truth through their, now timeless, examples. President Abraham Lincoln was one of the greatest leaders to have ever served as our country's commander in chief. He led the American people through some of our most difficult and formative years.

Early in Lincoln's life, he learned to never criticize. In fact, his criticism of an opponent in an open letter almost cost him his life, a lesson he would never forget. Lincoln's near-death experience taught him a valuable principle to live by; it taught him how to handle criticism.

During the intense pressures of the Civil War, President Lincoln received letters from statesmen, military generals, and constituents. They were scathing letters criticizing his actions leading up to and during the war. Upon receiving and reading the letters, Lincoln came up with a method for responding to his critics.

After President Lincoln was assassinated, an inventory of his office was performed. While cleaning out his desk, stacks of sealed, addressed, and mail-ready envelopes were found. They contained letters of response to the criticism he'd received during one of the most crucial periods in American history.

Lincoln knew that if he responded immediately, his response would likely only further incite his opponents, so he wrote responses to his critics and tucked them away in his desk for future review. I can only imagine that days later, after writing some of the responses, Lincoln might have opened them, made revisions, and sent them off. But most likely, after laying numerous letters of response to rest for a few days, he realized the majority of them did not need to be sent, which is why there were so many unsent letters found among his personal belongings.

Even though President Lincoln's life was tragically ended, he left behind a valuable lesson that has impacted many students of history, one that I have learned from and used and am grateful for.

Survey the Arena

In 1910, Theodore Roosevelt gave a speech in Paris, France, that ignited the crowd and left an indelible mark on history. Below is an excerpt from his speech, "Citizenship in a Republic," that has been famously named "The Man in The Arena."

> "It is not the critic who counts; not the man who points out how the strong man stumbles, or where the doer of deeds could have done them better. The credit belongs to the man who is actually in the arena, whose face is marred by dust and sweat and blood; who strives valiantly; who errs, who comes short again and again, because there is no effort without error and shortcoming; but who does actually strive to do the deeds; who knows great enthusiasms, the great devotions; who spends himself in a worthy cause; who at the best knows in the end the triumph of high achievement, and who at the worst, if he fails, at least fails while daring greatly, so that his place shall never be with those cold and timid souls who neither know victory nor defeat."[2]

This brilliant speech should be read every time a brave person in the arena encounters a critic.

Some Final Thoughts

Sometimes we need to receive criticism, and sometimes there is a need to give criticism. Regarding the latter, a quote from Anne Lamott can lend wisdom, "You don't always have to chop with the sword of truth. You can point with it, too."

Carefully constructed criticism delivered with good intent has the power to build up instead of tearing down.

In his book *The War of Art*, Steven Pressfield encourages, "The professional learns to recognize envy-driven criticism and to take it for what it is: the supreme compliment. The critic hates most that which he would have done himself if he had had the guts."[3]

Lastly, if you receive criticism that burns, take it, turn it around, and use it for some good. Let this be an encouragement to you to continue your race, art, business venture, memoir, or whatever it may be that you are passionately engaged in. Stay true to your mission and persevere, especially when you encounter a critic. Your work matters!

Challenges

*"Obstacles are those frightful things
you see when you take your eyes off
the goal." Henry Ford*

Challenges are a beautiful thing. They test us and allow us to grow to new levels of personal and professional success. Without challenges, we gradually sink into a state of paralysis. When our lives go without challenges, almost every aspect of them suffers from erosion.

Our bodies, minds, and spirits need new challenges, obstacles to break them down in order for them to become stronger, and without them, we slide into comfortability. The problem with comfortability is that its true state is one of decline. As the world, time, and people march forward, the comfortable are left behind. A mentor of mine once told me, 'The only way to coast is downhill.'

An obstacle-free life, however gradual, is terribly painful; it causes stagnation and eventual death to the warrior spirit, one that is all but gone in the modern day. Challenges, however, are what set hearts ablaze, send wandering souls on pilgrimages, fuel us with purpose to fight through terminal illness, dare the climber to free solo El Capitan or traverse the deadly wiles of the

Amazon River; they have the power to wake the near dead from their sleepy existence, and because of this— challenges should be seen as good and necessary for meaningful growth.

Physically, this concept is easy to prove out. Have you ever gotten into a workout routine in which you were exercising consistently? What happened when you missed a week? Muscles atrophied, slowly broke down, and their capacity for work was diminished. How about the first time you ran a mile or the first time you completed a set of ten pushups? Your body was challenged, and it grew to a new level of strength and stamina during recovery.

The same principle holds true for our mental faculties. Our minds grow when they are challenged with obstacles in learning—think of the first time you were introduced to algebra and your mind struggled to grasp what x represented. Your thinking was challenged to conceptualize solving for an unknown value, and it grew when it succeeded.

Similarly, the spirit can be broken down and built back up, just as the mind and body can. Prayer, meditation, and retreats of solitude can challenge the spirit. Have you ever not eaten for a few days, gone on a fast? Notice the terminology here—when we speak of a fast—we say, 'I am going on a fast' or 'I went on a fast.' Why? Because during a fast, the spirit travels somewhere, to a higher plane, to some new dimension. If you have 'gone on a fast' you know that it's brutally painful, but it does something to the spirit, cleans it out, recalibrates it. The human spirit is remarkable—it is stronger than our mind and body—it's what drives our mind and body to new heights, but only if we acknowledge its power and develop it by way of challenges.

Our response to challenges will largely determine the capacity of our mind, body, and spirit. If we view challenges as negative occurrences in life, we become stifled, and we self-impose a ceiling on our potential by settling into comfortability. But if we see challenges as opportunities to learn, grow, and innovate, our lives become limitless, and we enter into a new realm of possibility by moving from a fixed arena to an unbounded, exponential horizon.

Real breakthroughs happen when we notice the silver lining in each challenge; life-altering paradigm shifts can occur when we realize—every obstacle holds some type of reward in conquering it. Challenges are what sharpen the mind, body, and spirit into instruments of progress. Conversely, comfortability is the enemy of progress.

Leonardo da Vinci once shared, "It had long since come to my attention that people of accomplishment rarely sat back and let things happen to them. They went out and happened to things."[4]

The wisdom of Leonardo is something to pay attention to. In his day, he faced many cultural challenges. He was abandoned by his father a week after his birth and was considered a bastard because he was born out of wedlock, which in the fifteenth century was regarded as almost curse-like. Despite Leonardo's inherited challenges, he drove himself to become a polymath—an autodidact in science, art history, technology, and the humanities. The extent of his formal education ended in elementary, but he persevered and embraced the challenges his life and circumstances presented; taking pride in the fact that he was an underdog of sorts, he sought out apprenticeships and other nontraditional ways of learning.

Leonardo went on to paint the world's most famous and valuable art including the Last Supper, which depicts a great challenge in itself; the Vitruvian Man; the Salvator Mundi, a painting that sold for a record-setting $450.3 million, making it the most costly painting of all time; and, of course, the Mona Lisa, the most celebrated and renowned painting of all time.

We can learn from history and the formidable challenges it presented. When we see challenges as opportunities, as Leonardo did, we can begin to seek them out instead of avoiding them. History is replete with examples of people who decided to 'happen to things,' and in turn, they joined the pantheon of great artists, pioneers, and inventors now celebrated because of their marks on history. Their lives confirm 'Fortune favors the bold.'

Work

---

*"My experience has been that work is
almost the best way to pull oneself
out of the depths." Eleanor Roosevelt*

The average person spends most of their days on Earth engaged in some type of work. In general, we spend more time with coworkers than we do with our family members. The types of work we engage in have changed drastically, moving from the plow to the keyboard, as we have shifted from the agricultural and industrial ages to the information economy, or knowledge economy as some call it, but the amount of work we do and our dedication to it has not changed much over time.

There is something deep inside of us that knows we must work—that we can find progress and fulfillment through our labor. Our biological structure, at its most basic function, performs work; cells split and reproduce in order to grow. Similarly, the totality of our structure, our bodies, are designed for utility—to labor, to progress, to work.

Those who wake without the obligation of work find themselves, sooner or later, lacking purpose. Many times, if we are not careful, our work can become us. Often, when we meet someone for the first time we ask,

'What do you do?' A common reply is, 'I am a plumber, software engineer, or scientist (insert any other occupation here),' instead of 'I work in the field of plumbing,' and thus we have confused 'what we do' with 'who we are.' It is no wonder that our work, consuming most of our existence, mistakenly becomes who we are. However consuming, our work must never turn into our reason for living, which is dangerous because entire industries come and go, quickly nowadays. If our work becomes who we are, a part of our identity is at risk of being lost along with an industry or job.

The danger of attaching our identity to our work can have serious, sometimes even fatal, consequences. Some professions, such as those in fields of medicine, religion, the arts, and military service, are so rich in culture and indoctrination, the work is more likely to swallow the identity of the person whole if one is not prepared against it.

The medical student becomes the doctor, the army recruit becomes the soldier, and the young painter becomes the artist who is obsessed and will die trying to fulfill life's work. Why? Because the person no longer does the work, but instead has become the work—their profession has consumed them.

A healthy approach to work is to think of oneself as a contractor of their skills, experience, and labor. For example, I may contract my writing skills in the service of a publishing house. During that service, I render my writing service for a wage. When we look at our work as something separate from us, a service, it buffers us from becoming too attached to the work.

Work is a vital component to the foundation of our life, and when we understand that, we gain more than a wage for our work, we can gain some deeper level of gratification for it, since on some fundamental level, we were meant to work.

Albert Schweitzer, a polymath who was awarded the Nobel Peace Prize, lived by a code of service. He once shared, "I don't know what your destiny will be, but one thing I do know. The only ones among you who will be really happy are those who have sought and found how to serve."

Our work can intertwine with our purpose—service to others, without distorting our identity. It is a way we can touch lives and lift humanity to new heights, but the importance of work is too often mistaken as a necessary evil, a way to finance one's existence, a 'have to' instead of a 'get to.' A healthy view of work is to see it as inherently good because it fulfills a deep need for the worker and for society. Without work, both the worker and society begin to disintegrate.

Work brings the wage that supplies our life. Toil is a good thing because it brings in the harvest and provides the worker with a sense of significance. Without work, the body and mind wither. Still, many see work as a means to an end and fail to realize without work, our fulfillment, purpose, and even existence would be impossible.

The Herd

"Heaven knows, punishment and trance are a great deal more comfortable and familiar than aliveness." Anne Lamott

When we become stuck in life, it is because something—some idea, actual event, or assumed circumstance, maybe fear or some other exacerbated negative emotion—has convinced us we are no longer individuals, but just members of the herd—that we must act a certain way, avoid standing out, do our best not to offend, and stay cramped up in a mold that society wants to keep us in. This is a lie, maybe the mother of all lies; this is the herd mentality.

Moving in the same direction as everyone else seems safe on the surface, doesn't it? Traveling in a pack seems secure. If others are moving toward a common goal, it is probably a safe bet, so we tell ourselves.

The herd mentality goes something like this: get educated, find a secure job, work for the better part of a life, save for retirement, try to enjoy retirement, and then die.

Wow! Exhilarating, isn't it? There is nothing wrong with this mentality. After all, it is a proven path that most people are marching along.

But the problem with following the herd is that one of two things could and likely will happen. The first is, we could get slaughtered at any moment. Not literally, but economically. Not chopped up into Salisbury steaks. Remember those? Instead, at any moment, we could fall prey to a downsize, upshift, horizontal tilt or any other nebulous term used to explain we are no longer economically viable.

The second thing that could happen in the herd is we find a comfortable place to graze with a few other cows we can get along with, and we become comfortable. We chew grass and shoot milk out of the lower half of the factory, and we end up getting milked for all we are worth (metaphorically speaking).

The facts are: the herd moves when told to move, eats what it is given to eat, and produces according to market demands. The market dictates how much the herd produces and if the herd's product is a success or an abject failure.

When we are in the herd, we often get comfortable chewing on our standard fare (daily tasks and routines). We reject newness or innovation because, 'That's not the way we have done it in the past,' and we SETTLE in for the long haul.

Sound fun? Sound new? Sound risky? The answer is no to all, but very few will break out of the herd and make a decision to do something unique. Very few will be the rabble-rousers who say, 'Today is the day. No more grass for me. I am taking a leap of faith!'

Here's the silver lining or if you'd rather, the silver bullet—not the beer—the one that takes out the werewolf! We get to decide if we will continue cranking away day after day shooting milk out of our udders while grinding away following the herd.

We also get to decide if we will create a new industry or disrupt an old one! Don't believe me? Learn from a real-life example of herd disruption, the invention of almond milk.

Who knew almond milk would be a thing? Who knew an almond could be milked? Yet someone figured it out. Someone said, 'I will no longer be milked for all I am worth, nor will I be a Salisbury steak! Instead, I am going to milk almonds. Then I am going to sell a lot of almond milk and piss off a lot of cows. Mooo.'

Leaders are rebels who see the herd moving in one direction and realize there are 364 different directions to travel in. Hey, maybe you could produce peanut or cashew milk? Nope! Those are already a thing … who'd-a-thought they would've been a few decades ago?

Be a rebel. Step out of the herd. Do something remarkable!

Desperation

"The mass of men lead lives of quiet desperation." Henry David Thoreau

Desperation is the prime ingredient of a mediocre existence. To live in desperation, we must continue to bury our deepest desires—the very passions that bring us to life. To live in desperation, we ignore our greatest freedom, the freedom to become. To live in desperation, we surrender to living in the shadows of possibility.

What holds us back from seeing and acting on our true capability? What causes us to live in fear instead of possibility?

Is there something deep inside of you longing to get out? You were born unique—in fact you were born a specialist. No one on earth has the same combination of capabilities and talents you have. This fact makes your nature one of a kind, and for someone to imitate your nature would be futile. Likewise, for you to ignore your nature and desire to be someone else is counter to the very reason you exist.

Thomas Merton wrote, "Be yourself, everyone else is taken."

There is nothing more important and exceptional than becoming the 'You' that longs to get out and become known. But this is not how most live their lives. Henry David Thoreau's words stand true today:

"The mass of men lead lives of quiet desperation. What is called resignation is confirmed desperation. From the desperate city you go into the desperate country, and have to console yourself with the bravery of minks and muskrats. A stereotyped but unconscious despair is concealed even under what are called the games and amusements of mankind. There is no play in them, for this comes after work. But it is a characteristic of wisdom not to do desperate things."[5]

Have you ever witnessed someone step into their purpose and start living the life they desired to live? It's an amazing and beautiful thing. Regrets, fear, inhibition, lack, greed and many other self-afflictions begin to fade away when someone embraces who they were meant to be.

I witnessed a friend begin to share his art with the world. He had a talent that was locked deep inside of him for almost forty years. He's a very successful leader and has been for a very long time, but he failed to share what he was most passionate about with others for too long. When I told him that I took notice of his art (his true passion) and really liked it, he came alive and couldn't stop talking about how he had always wanted to paint, but for some reason he had repressed the desire for years.

My friend, who was locked in a battle of fear, was living out a shadow career that he used as an excuse to avoid the very passion that would bring him to life.

Finally, he began painting, but instead of sharing his work with the world, he hid his paintings in his garage for years without showing them to anyone. But then one day, he let his passion out, and it began to astonish the people around him. When he began sharing his passion for painting with the world, he became enlivened with purpose.

> *"The only thing we have to fear is fear itself." Franklin D. Roosevelt*

Fear shackles us and keeps us chained to a mere shadow of our true selves. It holds us back from moving in the direction that fulfills our hearts. Fear is a passion killer. However, when we begin to chase our dreams and passions, we realize that fear begins to dissipate naturally—that action dispels it.

Be bold and run toward your dreams. You were born with a unique blend of originality that is worthy of embrace, that needs to be shared with others.

Take that originality and create something beautiful; it is a gift you were born with on purpose.

Genius

---

*"Whatever you can do, or dream you
can do, begin it. Boldness has genius,
power, and magic in it."*
William H. Murray

Everyone has a genius lying inside of them waiting to be found. It waits for us to call it to our service, for its sole purpose is to serve us and others. This genius that resides in each of us is a special gift that was given to us by our Creator. It is a unique mixture of various abilities that form to help us stand apart as a powerful and creative individual. Until we find this genius, we can never fulfill our true purpose; therefore, it is imperative that we seek out and cultivate our genius.

There is a dangerous myth that confuses many, a belief that only select individuals have a special genius in them, but this is incorrect. We are all born unique but then as time passes, we are taught by society, culture, education, and other systems to become homogeneous. Many people look at others, those who have discovered their genius, and lavish them with praise and wonder how they became so talented, smart, or exceptional, but this too is a mistake. Instead we should take a deep look inside ourselves and search for the thing that sets us apart. When we find that gift, we have found our genius.

The word *genius* is defined by the Oxford dictionary as such: exceptional, intellectual, creative power, or other natural ability.

But let's look at the word's origin; it will give us a fuller understanding of its meaning.

The word originates in Late Middle English: from Latin, 'attendant spirit present from one's birth, innate ability or inclination.' The original sense, the 'spirit attendant on a person' gave rise to a sense 'a person's characteristic disposition' (late sixteenth century), which led to a sense 'a person's natural ability,' and finally, 'exceptional natural ability' (mid seventeenth century).[6]

> "The ancient Romans believed that every human baby was born with what they called his or her 'genius,' a guardian spirit assigned at birth. Roman birthday parties were held not so much to honor an individual as to honor that person's genius, the divine being that came into the world with him or her."[7]

It wasn't until the last century that we began to assign 'high intelligence' as a primary definition of genius. Usually one thinks of a phenom—a child prodigy, someone like Einstein, Beethoven, or even Michael Jordan—when they think of the word genius, so let's explore these individuals and look at how they achieved their title, their genius status.

It was at an age no later than five when young Einstein was given a compass by his father. It was this simple gift that sparked his curiosity and began what he called 'his moment of wonder.' He questioned how the needle of the compass could move without anything touching it and only a simple shift in direction. He concluded that "something deeply hidden had to be behind things."[8]

This moment of wonder led young Einstein to commit to learning about the 'deeply hidden,' the science behind things. His study of how things worked began as a young boy, and over his lifetime, he developed his genius, his curiosity and wonder. Einstein was not born with the theory of relativity embedded in his mind, nor was he born a Nobel Prize recipient, but instead, he identified his genius—a curiosity for how things worked—and then developed it. Finally, his genius rewarded him and those around him with its creativity and power.

Like Albert Einstein, Ludwig van Beethoven began the exploration and training of his genius at the young age of five. His father, Johann, also a musician, became his first teacher and quite possibly his harshest critic. Young Beethoven was pushed past his limits, which often brought him to tears during his lessons. Beethoven then trained under Christian Gottlob Neefe, another lifelong student of music who began composing his own music at the age of twelve. Neefe assisted Beethoven in producing his first pieces of music.

Decades later, just five years before Beethoven's principal instructor passed away, his pupil wrote to him from Vienna to promise, "Should I ever become a great man, you too will have a share in my success."[9]

Beethoven was born the son of a musician, began his training at age five, and was taught by one of the most notable instructors available. No doubt he was born with a seed of natural ability, 'his genius,' but it wasn't until he cultivated it, that it began to serve him and those around him.

Michael Jordan is arguably the greatest basketball player of all time. During his NBA Hall of Fame speech, he mentioned the sibling rivalry that helped him cultivate his genius at an early age. He said he was locked into competition with his brothers and sister since childhood, and that it drove him to new levels of success.

He then referred to Leroy Smith, the player who was chosen over him on the varsity basketball team. With a smile of admiration, he said:

> "And then there's Leroy Smith. Now you guys think that's a myth. Leroy Smith was a guy when I got cut he made the team—on the varsity team—and he's here tonight. He's still the same 6'7" guy—he's not any bigger—probably his game is about the same. But he started the whole process with me, because when he made the team and I didn't, I wanted to prove not just to Leroy Smith,

not just to myself, but to the coach that picked Leroy over me, I wanted to make sure you understood—you made a mistake dude."[10]

Jordan's defeat at an early age pushed him to try harder. There was no elusive genius that transported him to a pinnacle of success, instead, it was trial and error, defeat and triumph, belief in and the cultivation of his genius that went on to win him the nickname Air Jordan. He committed to not allowing any obstacle to stay in his way. Similarly, the sooner we believe in our genius and begin to cultivate it, the sooner we will experience our greatness.

Each person discovers their genius at different times and in different ways. It may happen when a child enrolls and begins training for a talent show. We see these types on reality television shows and wonder how they became so great. It may take others thirty years to discover their genius. The difference between one finding their genius at ten years old versus finding their genius at thirty years old, is the point in time one believes in and begins to cultivate their genius.

When we see the greats, those like Einstein, Beethoven, Jordan, and others who have made it to a pinnacle of success, sometimes we believe they were born gifted and did not have to cultivate their genius, but this thinking is a mistake of haste.

No one is born with a fully developed genius. It takes years of training the genius before it begins to serve them and others. The person who continues to train and sculpt their genius, prepares and exercises it, is the one who will be served by their genius.

William H. Murray, the Scottish expeditioner and prisoner-of-war writer, said it most eloquently:

> "Until one is committed, there is hesitancy, the chance to draw back .... Concerning all acts of initiative (and creation), there is one elementary truth, the ignorance of which kills countless ideas and splendid plans: that the moment one definitely commits oneself, then Providence moves too. All sorts of things occur to help one that would never otherwise have occurred. A whole stream of events issues from the decision, raising in one's favor all manner of unforeseen incidents and meetings and material assistance, which no man could have dreamed would have come his way.... Whatever you can do, or dream you can do, begin it. Boldness has genius, power, and magic in it. Begin it now."[11]

There is a seed of genius in each of us. Our objective, then, is to identify it and grow it into a mighty oak so that we can benefit from it and use it to serve others. Even the Holy Scripture affirms each of us was gifted like no other and that we should use our gift to serve others.[12]

Anger

---

*"Anger is often what pain looks like
when it shows itself in public."*
Krista Tippett

I remember walking down the hall of my home as a young kid, and every time I did, I was a little afraid because I caught a glimpse of the anger in the walls. Every few feet there was a hole in the wall, a place where my dad had punched through it. The walls reminded me of the times my dad lost his temper and, in a rage, let out a yell then smashed his fist through them. I now realize that every hole in the wall of my home was a manifestation of pain that my father was holding onto.

As a kid, I wrestled with a lot of pain and anger. I remember being locked in my room for days and sometimes weeks due to my bad behavior, a manifestation of my own pain. I would get so mad that I would pray that God would take me in my sleep. I wanted to go away to a place where there was no more pain, no more anger, and no more holes in the walls.

Around the age of eleven, I developed a nervous habit; it was a manifestation of the pain I was dealing with. I began to pick the middle knuckles of my fists.

It was an outlet of sorts, a method of soothing the way I felt on the inside.

One Sunday morning at church our Sunday school teacher asked the class a question. I knew the answer, so I raised my hand, and blood began to drip from my knuckle where I had nervously picked open the skin. A friend of mine got my attention and pointed out that my hand was bleeding. As soon as I noticed the blood dripping from my hand, I was ashamed because of the feelings attached to what was happening. I shrank back into my chair and tried to hide it. For years I hid my pain, but eventually, it turned to anger and caused pain to the people I cared most about and to myself.

Twenty-five years later, I still remember the holes in the walls of my home and the habit I developed to deal with my own pain. It is true that our deepest and most painful wounds often rear their ugly heads in the form of anger. Anger always causes more pain, and so the vicious cycle continues, like an unrelenting wave that never finishes crashing.

Just last week, I was so frustrated with my son that I smacked him on the back of his head. Nothing serious, just a little smack, so I thought. His response was, 'I always know when you are going to hurt me.'

The words from my son were sobering and painful. It felt like someone pulled my heart out and threw it against the floor. I was hit with immediate regret for what I did, but the thing is—actions can't be rewound, and sometimes their wake can be felt for a lifetime. They have staying power, just like the marks in the hall of my home as a kid. After a few minutes, I apologized to my son; he shrugged it off like it was no big deal, but it was, at least to me. I realized the vicious cycle of pain and anger that I saw in the walls of my home was still crashing in my life and now falling on my son.

I thought back to my childhood, to the years when my stepdad used to smack me in the back of my head when he got frustrated. It happened often, and his smacks were powerful enough to jar my head forward and sometimes leave pain in my neck. I must have been smacked a hundred times as a kid, and I cannot remember him apologizing once. More waves from my childhood were crashing in my life, their wakes reaching my son.

Reflecting on my past has helped me realize that I have allowed some of my painful experiences to manifest as anger. The beast of anger from my childhood still has its claws in me; they are now reaching for my kids, and it's up to me to figure out how to stop them. While reading a book by Robert Bly I came across a nugget of wisdom that encourages me and hopefully will encourage you too. Bly writes:

> *"Where a man's wound is, that is*
> *where his genius will be."*

If this is true, and I believe it is, there is hope, maybe even genius, somewhere in the depths of our pain.

Words

"The effect you have on others is the
most valuable currency there is."
Jim Carrey

Whether we know it or believe it, we all have a wildly powerful ability to take and give life with our words. Many people underestimate the power their words carry, and so they carry a destructive force.

Often, when I speak publicly, I ask the audience to close their eyes for one minute and think back to a time when someone said something that marked their life forever. I then ask the audience, 'By show of hands, how many of you remember someone saying something to you that marked you forever?' Invariably, every hand in the audience raises, indicating their lives have been permanently marked by the words of another. If you would like to prove this out, take a minute to ask and answer the question yourself.

This simple exercise reveals the extreme power a few words can hold, a power so great, they can mark the history of someone's life forever. But if we invert the question and ask, 'Have I ever said something that has marked the life of another person forever,' it becomes a little harder to answer. I would suggest the answer is most certainly, yes. The question then becomes: have our words marked the lives of others for better or for worse? When we realize the power we have in our words, we can begin to use them for good. There is a person who was written into one of the greatest stories, in my estimation, ever recorded. His name was Barnabas, and the meaning of his name was 'son of encouragement.' Another translation of his name meant 'son of consolation.' While it cannot be proven, I believe he was written into history because he carried out the meaning of his name and used his words to encourage and console others.

There are still people of this 'Barnabas' nature around today, but they are few and far between. My hope is that I can be seen as a son of encouragement over the course of my life because in our day and age, there is a destructive and pervasive narrative being communicated from the news outlets, the entertainment industry, the schoolyard bullies, and talking heads demanding our attention. The narrative tears people down, but each of us reading these words have the power to combat it.

While giving a commencement speech, Jim Carrey told the graduating class of Maharishi International University, "The effect you have on others is the most valuable currency there is."[13]

Much of the currency that will leave an effect on the lives of others will be transacted through our words. This concept is not novel, it has been passed down from antiquity. The ancient proverbs tell us, "Death and life are in the power of the tongue."[14]

This world needs more sons and daughters of encouragement, people like Barnabas, who give of themselves to lift the spirits of others. I will explain how and why everyone reading this can attempt to emulate Barnabas and become a son or daughter of consolation.

How to use your words powerfully and positively
Think of yourself as a modern-day farmer. I try to remind myself to act like one on a daily basis. What do farmers do? They plant seeds to yield future crops. The seeds that they plant go on to feed the lives of others, and our words have the power to do the same. When we use our words to encourage, it benefits us, the people they are planted in, and they begin to set an example for others to follow.

How we become modern day farmers with our words
We can select a few people daily that we will sow (plant) words of encouragement or consolation into. Use whatever method is appropriate for you. Here are a few that I use: letters, text messages, social media messages, endorsements, letters of recommendation, internet reviews, and good old-fashioned phone calls to let people know they are important.

The method does not matter as much as the message, the seed you plant. I would venture to say that everyone needs encouragement, and they desire it too, so when you select who you want to encourage, know it will be received well. Then go on to planting seeds of encouragement and watch the amazing things that grow from them.

Why you should use your words to plant seeds

Not only do people need and desire words of encouragement, but we as modern-day farmers will benefit from giving them. There is a timeless principle called the Law of the Harvest that says if we plant good seeds in good soil, we will reap a harvest. It is a biblical principle and a philosophical principle, so no matter your worldview, the principle holds true. If we plant good seeds, we will reap a harvest.

The harvest we reap may look obscure or come in an unexpected form, but the harvest is not the main objective, it's a fringe benefit. The main objective is to plant good seeds and become a modern-day Barnabas, a son or daughter of encouragement, to others because this world needs it. You now have the understanding, power, and responsibility, if you accept it, to become an encourager.

Forgiveness

"If you wish to travel far and fast, travel light. Take off all your envies, jealousies, unforgiveness, selfishness, and fears." Glenn Clark

What an incredible idea—the more we free ourselves of the heavy baggage of anger and hurt, and all of their ugly cousins, the farther and faster in life we will travel. The opposite is true also. Unforgiveness is the mother of resentment, and there is no better analogy to explain resentment than to compare it to poison. When we resent someone, it is like drinking poison and wishing it to harm the person we are angry with. It's not only self-harm, but it's also desiring harm on others, which is why unforgiveness is so dangerous, even toxic at times.

As we layer on unforgiveness and the resentment that accompanies it, we contribute to our own undoing. If it persists, the damage from unforgiveness and resentment quickly outweighs the pain from our offender. This happened with me for too long; I was a victim of my anger and unforgiveness. They fueled my emotions while I spun my wheels for years, never traveling forward. While I was weighed down by unforgiveness, life continued to march on … time and tide wait for no man.

When we fail to forgive, in effect, we emotionally travel backward, bypassing the growth that comes from reconciliation and healthy relationships. In a state of unforgiveness, it's hard to see what is going on because when we are full of resentment, we become self-absorbed, caught in a snare of self-destructive thinking, and until we break free from all the thoughts that bear down on us, we are stunted from progress.

To move forward, we must forgive. We must come to terms with the brokenness of humanity and the fact that everyone fails from time to time. It is true that hurting people, hurt people. This becomes a self-perpetuating cycle, broken only by forgiveness, by laying down our sword of retaliation.

When we lay down our pain and trade it for forgiveness, we release the baggage that weighs us down; only then can we begin to experience freedom. By putting down the poison of resentment, we unshackle ourselves and are able to live and grow emotionally. When we forgive, we take on new life and a greater capacity to love those around us, the ones who need us most.

Maya Angelou wisely taught, "Forgiveness is a gift you give yourself."

Forgiveness allows us to share our greatest gift with others. It allows us to share our love again.

Good and Evil

*"The line separating good and evil
passes ... right through every human
heart" Aleksandr Solzhenitsyn*

The line between good and evil is thin, elusive at times, and mysterious; it runs directly through the heart of every man. Good and evil wage war first on the battleground of hearts. The victor travels from the hearts to the actions of people. Evil is deceptive, sometimes it masks itself as good.

Good and evil take forms in our society that are too often misunderstood. It is hard, maybe even impossible, to say, 'this or that is good or bad,' without coloring in broad strokes of judgment in an attempt to help us easily understand the most complex matters.

Many things we call 'bad' or 'evil' are mistaken strawmen we build out of our emotional desire to be good, just in thinking, or to defend those ideas and people we care about, those we see persecuted and alienated. A 'strawman,' in this context, is something that lacks real substance, a false identity, or misattributed association. A strawman argument is created to deceive, but a strawman in this context is an idea or conclusion we jump to out of emotional intensity, and in haste, sometimes out of a desire to do good, we miss the mark completely due to our misconceptions, prejudices, or lack of experience.

What we fail to realize is the source of evil is always born in the heart first, never in an amoral object, institution, race, or government, even though at times throughout history all of these things have been labeled as 'evil.' We, at times, in an attempt to right injustices, have forced wills, emotions, and personalities on things that are incapable of having them, in turn propping up strawmen, sometimes without even knowing it.

I recently decided to introduce my seven-year-old son to his first shooting experience. I told him, 'We are going on an adventure together.' We began by taking a trip to Walmart. I explained that we needed supplies before our trip as we walked toward the sporting goods section and picked up a pack of BBs. I announced, after a questioning look from my son, 'We are going shooting together.'

His reaction was one of fearfulness; he saw guns nearby and became reluctant. The reason for his fear became apparent when he said, 'A gun killed my teacher's dog.'

After we checked out and got in the car, I set a course for the Sam Houston National Forest, which is about thirty miles north of where we live. My son began asking, 'Can I just shoot a Nerf gun dad?'

I realized that first, before shooting a real gun, my son needed a lesson on good and evil.

I said, 'Guns do not kill people—only people kill people.' I explained that a person using a weapon killed his teacher's pet, not a gun. I did my best to explain that guns, just like any other inanimate object, a stick or rock, or even a knife, have no will, emotion, or moral ability, that weapons of any type, be they guns or swords, are lifeless until used by a moral being, and only then can they be used for both good and evil.

Nobel Prize-winning author, Aleksandr Solzhenitsyn, wrote,

> "The line separating good and evil passes not through states, nor between classes, nor between political parties either – but right through every human heart – and through all human hearts. This line shifts. Inside us, it oscillates with the years. And even within hearts overwhelmed by evil, one small bridgehead of good is retained."[15]

When emotions flare and rage, they charge our judgment, deceiving it at times. Just the other day, while discussing our next family vacation, I told my wife I didn't want to visit France because its people are of a certain ideology. But after catching myself using sweeping judgments about an entire population I am relatively unfamiliar with, I began to do some research, and I realized my judgment was from misunderstanding.

The danger of misunderstanding 'good' and 'evil' and where they come from is a very serious idea because of the implications it carries. If we are not careful, we can mistakenly project one person's or group's actions onto an entire population or nation. Undoubtedly, this has led to catastrophic events in our history—wars, riots, and racism. One person's vile heart and action have the power to corrupt the views of many.

Did you know that Adolf Hitler, first, before waging a war that led to the extinction of millions, wanted to become an artist? The war between good and evil that raged in his heart was won out by the latter. His evil actions led to the destruction of nations, people groups, and marked history with a stain so reprehensible, we still feel its aftershock today.

Personal sovereignty of the heart, the battleground where good and evil collide, must be fought for because the line between good and evil runs directly through every human heart.

Gardening

---

*"The revelation of thought takes men
out of servitude into freedom."*
Ralph Waldo Emerson

In 1903, James Allen published *As a Man Thinketh*, a short book of wisdom. It's based on the principle that our lives are a product of our own design. The book is simple, small, and valuable. If one can grab onto the concepts laid out in the tiny book of wisdom, it will help them live a life by design. Because of its vast importance, I will summarize a key lesson from the book with a story.

I was reminded of the book when my backyard began to go wild. I live in South Texas, a plush area of the country, where all sorts of things spring from the ground and grow. One morning, I noticed a weed sprouting just outside of my kitchen window. Over the next few days, I learned it was no normal weed; instead, it was a species of superweed that grew ten times stronger and faster than the nearby shrubbery and the rest of my yard.

Out of pure laziness, I neglected it, and for the next few weeks, I eyed it every time I went to my kitchen sink. Day after day, I made the standard trips to my kitchen to make coffee, fix meals, and wash a dish or two, only to find the rogue weed growing stronger and faster, haunting me with every peek in its direction.

I began to grow angry at the seasons, at the state of Texas, and at myself for allowing the superweed to grow and become an eyesore outside of my kitchen window. Admittedly, I was experiencing an irrational anger; nonetheless, it was a real source of frustration. With every passing day, the weed seemed to taunt me with its size and unsightly appearance. I watched as barbs and spiny leaves grew and flourished, reaching skyward, goading me toward madness through my window.

Over time, the superweed called other weeds to grow near it, like a strong military commander might call in reinforcements; however, the smaller weeds were dwarfed by the master's presence and dominating features—they were mere pawns compared to the superweed.

Finally, I snapped … I'd had enough. I had allowed this weed to grow in my yard, and simultaneously, without much awareness, to grow in my heart and mind. Anger welled up in me every time I walked into my kitchen. Enough was enough, so on one sunny Saturday afternoon, I pulled the lawn equipment out of the shed and handled the superweed, along with its army of dwarf clones taking root in my yard, seemingly prepping some sort of coup.

The first thing I did was don a pair of sturdy leather gloves; I reached for the root of the massive weed, took hold of it and ripped it from my yard, but the base of it snapped just above the ground. The roots of the weed were so strong, they remained rooted in the soil, and only time will tell if the freak weed will make a villainous comeback.

I tell you this simple story to share a powerful truth, one about the way our minds work. Oftentimes, we allow a small idea to corrupt a large territory of our mind. A singular thought can take root in our mind and heart, similar to the superweed that grew, plaguing my yard for weeks, growing out of control. Before we know it, the small thought has become a destructive force, taking up time, energy, and space that could have otherwise been used for profitable thoughts.

The wise person will take stock of her mind, her garden of thoughts, the most precious plot of space under her control.

She will tend her thoughts daily, pulling up the bad thoughts and watering good ones—thoughts that will grow into future productive crops. When she recognizes a weed, a poison in her thoughts, she will attack it when it is young—just take its root, rip it up, and dispose of it. If she tends the garden of her mind, she will enjoy the peace that accompanies a well-maintained life.

Love

"Love is always a risk, it's daring;
without courage, it's impossible."
Terry Weaver

Love is the strongest human emotion, greater than fear, anger, and jealousy combined. It is so powerful, it can heal wounds, unite hearts, and radically transform lives for the better. Love happens to be our greatest need in life; it's what causes the young girl to begin planning her wedding at age seven and what propels the young man to stand off on the schoolyard to defend his sweetheart.

Poets write about it, sculptors and painters show it with their hands, movies depict it in most of their narratives, wars are waged in lack of it, bridges are built to recapture it, cultures and societies ascend on it, and histories are repaired through it. To deny its power is impossible, I would argue, because humans are designed for it—to give and receive it.

Love, being our greatest need and desire, is paradoxical in nature; it's not truly attainable without another. It must be shared and returned. It's like the point where a river meets an ocean. The force of the two coming together continually exchanging power, pushing, sharing, giving and taking from one another. If force is lost from either source, there is a vacuum. In the same way, love without exchange of power, in isolation, cannot exist. It slowly dissipates without another.

It is also true that to be loved and to fully love, we must open ourselves up to the possibility of broken heartedness. Unrequited love is the most painful emotion one can experience, so love is always a risk … it's daring; without courage, it's impossible. Despite the risk, we can trust that love has the power to fill in the deepest valleys of pain with healing.

Love can be confused and imitated. Many talk of their affection by saying, 'I love you.' Fewer show their affection by *doing* 'I love you,' acting it out. Since love is an action, words are merely a reminder of something once done because true love, the kind that carries power, compels one to action. When true love is felt, it can't be mistaken by words.

I often remind my kids of my love with words. Their responses vary from, 'Love you too dad,' to 'I know dad,' and sometimes my reminder is met with a simple nod of acknowledgement. But when I show them my love, their responses are much different. When I throw a football with my son, he responds with a massive hug, a kiss, and a boisterous shout, 'I love you, dad,' a reminder of his love.

When I take my daughter on a date to a fancy restaurant and treat her like the princess she imagines herself as, she responds with a heart-melting smile and tiny arms wrapped around my neck. Even after weeks have passed, she reminisces, 'Remember when we went on that date to ….' Her response is a memory that lasts, tapping her shoulder every now and then to remind her of the treasure she is.

The act of love is powerful, mighty and gentle at the same time. Love elicits response, calling out for a return of its own kind; love self-perpetuates and becomes a creative force—it leaves marks in the memories of others, reminding them they are close to, at times inside of, another's heart.

The greatest acts of love transcend time and space—they become unleashed into some greater sphere of existence and are so ravenous, they destroy evil and consume pain. They are powerful enough to mark history because of their magnitude of sacrifice.

The great acts of love touch our hearts, wrapping them with some mysterious power—think of Martin Luther King Jr., Mother Teresa, and Jesus of Nazareth. These beloved figures lived out their love, a sacrificial love so great, it became them. Their lives became great love stories—so powerful, they have no ending. Each of these great love stories, with every telling, reverberates through the hearts of their hearers calling out for a response.

We too can love like this, but it will take a commitment. It will take a willingness to give and an understanding that in the end, we may be hurt, but love and the power it carries is worth the risk. To live a fulfilled life, we must believe that love is the most powerful action we are capable of and make a decision to use it for good.

Seeking

"What you seek is seeking you."
Rumi

What are you seeking? This question can reveal a lot about the story we are writing with our lives. Many seek things they can hold in their hands, items they can count or lock away and peek at every once in a while, to remind them of their worth. Think about this—what does society portray as rich? Big houses, money, status symbols like fancy cars, and jewelry, these are all ideas of importance in postmodern society. Are these things valuable in your life? What are you seeking?

Where do valuable relationships rank in what you are seeking? How about wisdom, knowledge, truth, and experience? These are things you cannot put in a safe, assign a monetary value to, or flash in front of a crowd … 'Hey take a look at my relationships!' Ever heard that on someone's list of bragging rights?

Consider this: most people seek things they can touch, count, protect, and admire. It is somewhat paradoxical that we tend to value things we cannot keep, things which are quickly forgotten toward the end of our lives.

The thirteenth-century Persian philosopher Rumi said, "What you seek is seeking you." This is why the question, 'What am I seeking,' is so vitally important to ask.

Have you heard the saying, 'hearses have no hitches?' It is true, at the end of our life we can take no possession with us—coffins are not built with luggage compartments. We have all witnessed the scene in a movie of a typical funeral where the officiator lists what has been left behind by the person who has passed. Invariably, it is a list of people, a spouse and maybe a few children, grandchildren and maybe even some friends if they were lucky. A list of things one can touch is never mentioned.

Kevin Kelly, the wise man that he is, identifies one thing we might take with us. He says, "When you die you take absolutely nothing with you except your reputation."

But is this the case? Maybe. Our reputation could be what is etched as our epitaph. We certainly have the opportunity to leave a reputation behind. It is what is idealized in the minds of those who remember us. A reputation is the sum total of the memories of a life in the minds of others. If we choose to idolize things, we forfeit leaving memories of true value behind in our reputation. But when we focus on people, meaningful ideals, and doing good to others, our reputation is crystalized in the minds of those we are closest to.

Consider this ancient proverb: "Acquire wisdom; and with all your acquiring, get understanding. Prize her, and she will exalt you; she will honor you if you embrace her. She will place on your head a garland of grace; she will present you with a crown of beauty."[16]

Is it paradoxical that what most people spend their entire lives seeking—possessions, money, toys, things—vanishes the second they pass and is not even mentioned when their life is spoken of at their final send-off.

So, what are we seeking? Or maybe a better question is, what should we be seeking? Should we not be seeking relationships, knowledge, wisdom, and experiences with those we care deepest for? These are things we cannot store up, count, or sell, but in the end, they are what matter most; they will bring true satisfaction and meaning to us and the lives we touch.

Perfection

> *"It's more important to know where you are going than to get there quickly. Do not mistake activity for achievement." Isocrates*

Perfection is an illusion. It is a mental trap that keeps people comfortably snuggled up with the status quo and afraid of chasing their dreams. On its face, 'perfect' seems like a noble idea—something we should long for. Continuous improvement, never settling, presenting the best self, and working hard until things are just right are all shadow forms of perfection. The ideas and their pursuit can be good as long as we know the difference between striving for growth and striving for perfection.

Under the veil perfectionism wears to disguise its deceptiveness lie conditions and ideas born out of fear and the need for approval. They are subtle and cunning, but potent nonetheless, quietly whispering in the back of our minds, 'If I am not perfect, what will everyone think of me?' In the end, perfectionism is a self-defeating idea because it is not humanly possible.

I sat down with a young man in his early thirties who was trapped in the rat race. He explained that by all measures of modern success he should have been happy. 'I have four kids, a beautiful wife, a high paying job, and a big home, but still there is something missing.'

He went on to share that he'd worked himself into the ideal situation, a position that others would kill for, but that he had dreams of doing something much different. He began to lay out his plans for pursuing his dreams, which included starting a consulting company that would fund the idea he really wanted to birth, a coaching company aimed at helping others create great lives for themselves. When I asked him what was holding him back, he explained, 'I work sixty hours per week and have no time for any pleasure, no time for my wife and kids, and no time for myself.'

This poor fellow was strung out with a job he did not like, leveraged to the hilt with a lifestyle that society deemed "successful," not able to spend time with the ones he loved because he was working sixty hours per week. All the while, most of what consumed his thoughts was breaking free from the life he'd constructed. The "perfection" didn't stop there. He topped things off by telling me that his marriage was on the rocks.

I challenged his plan by asking, 'Why don't you chase your dream directly? Start your dream company instead of some side company you hope will someday fund your dream?' His laundry list of excuses was typical. Have you heard these excuses? 'No money, no time, no family support, bad timing, unsure of the market, wife doesn't like it, …' the list goes on, ad infinitum.

Unfortunately, my friend fell into a trap that many fall into. He'd constructed such an elaborate plan, a plan so rife with complication and tangential direction, that in effect, it created a barrier between him and his dream. I call this a Triangulation Fallacy—someone desires to get to a certain point, let's call it Point-C, but instead of creating a plan to get there directly, they place artificial barriers in their path. They over-engineer their plans and end up designing a self-defeating strategy.

Why do people do this? Because they are afraid of failing if they were to chase their dreams directly. To clarify this idea let me elaborate. A hopeful dreamer of any kind, entrepreneur, writer or painter, musician, or aspiring world traveler, wants to get to Point-C, but they believe they must first go from Point-A, where they are now, to Point-B, a place they do not want to go or have any intention of staying. All the while, their dream of someday getting to Point-C is put on hold as they become entangled in a poorly constructed plan. Traveling to Point-B first is a fear-borne escape from pursuing a linear path to Point-C, the dream.

This Triangulation Fallacy is an illusion that stems from the idea of perfection—waiting for the perfect time, condition, security, et cetera, and it is a trap. The person who has a dream or desire but believes any form of perfection is a prerequisite of it, sabotages himself because deep down, somewhere in his psyche, is the worry the dream is not good enough or not worthy.

My friend and others who are tricked by perfectionism create elaborate plans that hold them back from what would truly fulfill them.

The person struggling with perfectionism should consider making a decision to pursue 'the dream' directly, then make some progress toward that dream daily. Dreams that are realized over long periods of stacking up daily wins, moving toward a dream persistently—despite imperfect conditions—will, over time, pay off.

Never aim for perfectionism; it's a fool's aim that is missed every time because perfection does not exist.

Mental Maps

"Life can only be understood backwards; but it must be lived forward." Soren Kierkegaard

Before we change anything, we must first have a basic understanding of the way it works. The mind is constantly at work organizing, filtering, and preparing for unknowns, by projecting, comparing, and analyzing. One way it accomplishes this important task is by creating mental maps.

Every time we have an experience or learn something significant, our brain adds a placeholder, a grouping of information, on our mental map. To get a better visual, we might compare it to a freeway system that has intersections, warning signs, directories, on- and off-ramps, and as we travel throughout our days, we refer to our map and the information it holds. We use this mental map to process old decisions, make new ones, and predict what may happen in the future.

Take a minute to think of the signs that exist on your mental map, both good and bad.

Some of the most powerful signs on our mental maps come from actions and words of others. These mental markers on our map are often the product of both good and bad experiences in our life that influence our current and future decisions. These signs on our mental maps have the ability to drastically impact the way we think about ourselves and treat others, so it is good to understand how they work. A good sign, or mental marker, from the past may be a promotion or bonus received—a medal awarded to us for meritorious work, maybe a state championship trophy or something of the like. A negative sign, however, may be planted when someone says something destructive like, 'You will never be a good singer, playwriter, musician, artist, and so forth.'

These significant events, both good and bad, have the tendency to place larger than normal signs on our mental maps, similar to the signs on the Las Vegas Strip that flash, change color, dance about, and demand our attention disproportionately compared to other signs. These are the ones that try and take control of our mind, and the only way to prevent that is to know how they work.

While the less significant experiences—the smaller signs on our maps—often live in the subconscious, sometimes going completely unnoticed but still having some influence on our psyche, the larger signs are what cause us to make hasty decisions or shrink in fear. Our decisions and perceptions are always biased, and to some degree controlled, by our mental maps.

A decade ago, I began to notice upon waking in the morning that negativity and fear were the first emotions and thoughts to flood my mind. It seems that the negative signs on our mental maps become the mind's default, the instinctual setting for the human mind. Our brain sends us messages about potential threats; they vary from 'disease runs in the family lineage' to 'fear of not having a job in the near future.' These are signals from the most powerful signs on our mental map, planted from experiences, a death in the family or stories about the great depression. Oftentimes they are temporary or misplaced signs.

Our mental maps and the signs they hold can come from all sorts of sources including books, entertainment, and cultures we live in. One primetime news segment can plant dozens of negative signposts. A political debate can plant another dozen; a story from a friend about a neighboring country's rise in poverty or drug war can plant a few more, and before we know it, we have a few hundred negative signposts on our mental map.

The negative signposts, which are the most prevalent in today's culture, have the ability to dig into our psyche, like the talons of a hungry falcon on fresh prey. When these negative ideas set in, they begin to cause a chronic state of anxiety in the mind and can have a drastic impact on our quality of life.

According to Psychology Today, news programming uses a hierarchy to determine which segments to run on the air. At the highest level lies the criteria 'if it bleeds, it leads.' This is what is known as fear-based news programming; it has two aims. The first is to grab the viewer's attention. In the news media, this is called the teaser. The second aim is to persuade the viewer that the solution for reducing the identified fear will be in the news story. If a teaser asks, 'What's in your tap water that YOU need to know about?' a viewer will likely tune in to get the up-to-date information to ensure safety.[17]

Additionally, Hollywood studios, radio stations (where the term shock jock originated—see Howard Stern or the late Don Imus), and marketers selling corporate America's products all understand the powerful idea that fear sells. These empires of influence wielders use this little-known fact about the mind to hustle, induce fear, and cajole you and I to latch onto fear-based narratives, ones that create addiction and anxiety until a fix is found.

There are many things we can do to combat the negative signposts that flood our mind constantly, oftentimes warping our thoughts and perceptions for days, weeks, years, and even entire lifetimes. Our mind is fertile ground for ideas of any nature, so here are a few solutions that can guard us from these mental threats. We can either close off certain channels of information to protect it, or we can offset our mental map's negative signs with positive ones. To close off a channel takes just cancelling our cable or shutting down our social media intake for a certain period of time.

After assessing our mental maps and determining the amount of work that needs to be done to get them to a healthy place, we may also need to be a little more proactive. We can do this by placing more good signs on our maps through positive affirmations, self-help literature, meditation, or prayer, all of which will begin to rebuild the healthy infrastructure in our mind. Adding new positive signs to our mental maps is important because our minds tend to default to a negative setting, one of survival, scarcity, and fear.

A simple but effective technique we can use to place good signs on our mental maps is to journal positive affirmations. Here is how to start: take a plain journal or notebook and record five positive things, people, or experiences in your life each morning before you start your day. I write about the big things I often take for granted: my family's health, my personal relationships, my freedom to choose, et cetera.

This powerful exercise can help us reinforce the positive and offset the negative signs in our mind, the ones that direct and control our thinking, emotions, and actions. By doing this exercise and by being aware of our mental maps, we can begin to think more clearly, make better decisions, and view life through a more precise and unbiased view.

Worship

---

*"A person will worship something ...
Therefore, it behooves us to be
careful what we worship, for what we
are worshipping, we are becoming."*
Ralph Waldo Emerson

One of the best ways to take inventory of what we are worshipping is to survey our bank account and our calendar. We spend time and money on the things we worship. As we worship things, we inadvertently or intentionally put blinders on to block out other things in life.

Our desire to worship, I believe, is woven into our DNA. We were made with an ability to focus our passion and time on things and people of our choosing. Have you ever gazed at a work of art, then revisited it to admire its beauty? Or have you ever heard a song from your favorite artist and then replayed it a couple hundred times before it became no longer worship worthy?

Merriam-Webster defines worship as: extravagant respect or admiration for or devotion to an object of esteem.[18]

Does this definition help you recall something you have worshipped in the past? I have worshipped many things: fame, money, self, but finally came to realize these idols lured me into unhappiness and a need for a new idol.

Most often, people worship money or self, both equally frustrating and pointless. After my own struggles with these forms of worship, I've come to believe they are the most destructive of idols. I will handle these two forms of worship separately to expose the downfall in the pursuit of them.

First, money. Many people believe that money and the attainment of it will solve their problems. And when the chase for it is over, either through exhaustion or surrender, people realize the pursuit of money is as vain as chasing a shadow.

Andrew Carnegie warned that there is nothing more debasing than the worship of money and that amassing wealth is one of the worst species of idolatry. Carnegie cautioned against Mammonism, the worship of money and possessions. Carnegie became one of the wealthiest men of all time, and after he learned the pitfalls of amassing wealth, he worked for the rest of his life to give his possessions away.[19]

Carnegie finally understood what the ancient Roman philosopher Seneca meant when he said, "These individuals have riches just as we say that we 'have a fever,' when really the fever has us."

If one's happiness is tied to their bank account or the stock market, they may be worshiping money, which the annals of history teach us always leads to unhappiness.

Self-worship is Mammon's greatest rival. Those who self-worship blind themselves from the beauty of others, relationships, and the wonder around them. The self-worshipper's highest form of praise is found in the mirror or the selfie. Time eventually conquers those who worship self in one of two ways, death or undoing, but it is a slow and painful battle, hard to break free from because self-worship assumes happiness can be found in isolation.

The worship of self is often a manifestation of atheism. Through all sorts of elaborate reasoning, atheism claims there is no God, but at its core is the understanding—if God exists, man, more specifically self, cannot be the superior being. Self-worship is most often nothing more than a prideful attempt to play God.

Atheism and self-worship have their roots in Gnosticism, which proliferated in the second century. Gnostics believed they had the ability to transcend and become god-like, moving from the material world to the spiritual world through acquisition of ever-increasing enlightenment via esoteric knowledge (gnosis).[20]

At the center of self-worship is delusion, isolation, and loneliness, three forces that war against relationships which hold meaning to life. In the heart of the self-worshipper there is always an unwinnable battle with pride being waged, which makes self-worship, like the worship of money and possessions, a futile pursuit.

Between 1646 and 1647, the Westminster Shorter Catechism produced a document containing 107 questions and answers. These questions were ones of deep human curiosity that had gone unanswered for many years. The most popular of the questions was, 'What is the man's chief end?' Essentially, this group of laypeople and theologians was attempting to explain why man exists. Their answer was, 'To glorify God.' The group then popularized the theological statement, "Man's chief end is to glorify God and to enjoy him forever."[21]

I list this option, of worshipping God, for the sole purpose of giving another option to an age-old human struggle. If worship is in fact woven into our design on some cellular level, then we will always be worshipping something. The question that each person must ask then becomes, 'Is the thing I am worshipping worthy, and is it that which I desire to become?'

"A person will worship something … Therefore, it behooves us to be careful what we worship, for what we are worshipping, we are becoming." Emerson

What are you worshipping?

Identity

---

*"The privilege of a lifetime is being
who you are." Joseph Campbell*

Some of the most uncomfortable and tragic times in my life have been when I defined who I was, my identity, through some presumed lens of those around me, by some potential circumstance I had no control over. I allowed my surroundings and misfortune to create a false identity.

I think back to my time in high school, when I lived in a trailer park and tried to hide the fact from everyone I knew because of my insecurities. What people might think shaped how I presented myself to the world. I was inverting my identity, and instead of being me, I tried to be an ideal version of what others might want. This was a very painful way to live and was a trap.

During my junior year, I had a couple of really good-hearted friends who offered to drive me home from school, which was about a two-mile trek. Instead of having them drive me all the way home, I asked them to drop me off at a friend's house a block away from where I lived. When my friends drove away and were out of my view, I walked home.

That walk home became a walk of shame for me. This roundabout guise was something I did because I was worried my friends might stop liking me based on where I lived. My identity was severely misplaced, and unfortunately this mistaken identity phenomenon is a common occurrence in the lives of many, one that can swallow up years and even decades sometimes.

This type of thinking, forming our identity based on what others might think of us, is especially dangerous because it keeps us in a posture of fear, one that seeks identity in someone else. This becomes a dangerous dance, a psychological concoction of attempted but impossible mindreading and acting out a false self.

The reason this is such a tragic mistake is because while we are spending time worried about what others may be thinking and allowing those thoughts to distort our identities, we also keep ourselves from what we could become.

A real paradigm shift happens when we move from having a false identity to a state of self-development. This transformation happens when we no longer allow thoughts of others, real or perceived, to affect who we are becoming. The phrase, 'who we are becoming,' is important to understand because it is largely based on individual choices we make in life.

One of the paramount choices we will make in life by abdication or self-actualization is determining who will form our identity. By abdicating our identity to others, we become people pleasers and our identities are never secure, because they are based on things outside of our control. Conversely, when we self-actualize, we take responsibility and control of who we are becoming.

Over a decade ago, I found a mug with a quote from an unknown author on it that said, "Life isn't about finding yourself, it's about creating yourself."

The mug is in my office and serves as a daily reminder of the choice I have in my becoming, that my identity is something not determined in finding, but rather, it is something I am day-by-day creating.

We will never be able to force a perception of ourselves in another's mind, but we can always work on who we are and believe that every experience and circumstance has taught us something of value, that nothing is wasted.

In psychology, there are two ideas that help us understand sovereign ability or lack thereof. The first is *the external locus of control*, the idea that the environment surrounding an individual and the things that happen to a person will decide who he or she becomes. Alternatively, *the internal locus of control* is the idea that a person has sovereign control of his or her thoughts and actions, thus the person can determine the outcome of his or her life.

The view one adopts regarding their *locus of control* will determine if their identity is self-created or sought after in external things.

Have you heard the term *victim mentality*? Those who suffer with the victim mentality view what happens through a filter—one that perceives tragedies, inequities, and circumstances of this world as happening to them, thus they are beholden to victimhood. The victim mentality is a trap that usually consumes and destroys one's life. Why? Because life is tough and unfair, and those who ascribe to the victim mentality have no control in life. Those afflicted with the victim mentality consequently skirt responsibility and become victimized by circumstance; they are imprisoned by everyday life.

However, if we adopt the idea that we have choice, that we are agents in our becoming, we can build a healthy identity. Instead of passively collecting an identity or seeking one out from external things, we can actively work to improve our futures and begin to see life as a set of lessons and opportunities to improve through, instead of oppressions.

It is unlikely we will be able to see our life as a gift until the previous decisions are made. When we begin to think of life as a set of choices that we have significant power over, we can view our present and future states as opportunities to flourish.

Now, when I do interviews about being a writer, I often include the fact that I was raised in a trailer park. It's a part of my past, something I had no control over—one that taught me a valuable lesson about my identity. But more importantly, I use it to encourage others that no matter where one comes from, the present and future are yet to be determined.

Our identities and who we become are always left to choices: we can choose to find ourselves in the opinions of others, or we can choose to forge ourselves from within.

> *"The thing that is really hard, and*
> *really amazing, is giving up on being*
> *perfect and beginning the work of*
> *becoming yourself."*
> *Anna Quindlen*

The Mind

*"Life is a process of becoming, a
combination of states we have to go
through. Where people fail is that
they wish to elect a state and remain
in it. This is a kind of death."*
Anaïs Nin

I heard it said that the greatest battle we will ever fight is
the one that rages in our mind. There, we face our
toughest enemies: self-doubt, depression, anger, past
experiences, broken narratives, and other self-defeating
ideas—some planted by ourselves and some planted by
others. The mind is a warzone. In it, thoughts lay
bludgeoned, our confidence is slain, and past mistakes
linger, wreaking havoc on the present. It is a dangerous
and sometimes dark place, but it is also the most worthy
territory to fight for.

If we desire to live with significance, we must suit up
daily in our battle gear and first defeat the enemies that
lurk in our mind, the devils of self-doubt. This battle
must be won before we can contribute meaningfully and
confidently to ourselves and those around us. A healthy
way to start each day is with an inspection and cleansing
of our thoughts, because (and this is very important) we
cannot believe everything we think.

Negative thinking is a self-fulfilling prophecy and is the mind's default setting, but we can do things to combat it. There are many ways to cultivate a positive mindset, but for the sake of practicality and brevity, I will share only a few.

The first way to cultivate a positive mindset is to destroy negative thoughts at their source. We cannot let bankrupt people and ideas live rent-free in our mind. The space in our mind is too valuable, even sacred, so we must reserve its use for good ideas and people only. A good landlord knows his tenants; he keeps the good ones and evicts the bad ones. Likewise, we should constantly inventory and clear the corrupt tenants and ideas from our mind. This practice will manifest in our physical life when we practice it daily.

Another way to cultivate a healthy mindset is by planting good ideas in our mind, ones that will eventually yield good thoughts and develop into valuable harvests. The best way I have found to plant good seeds in the mind is by searching for and studying truth.

The source of truth I study on a daily basis is the Bible. It can be controversial, and it can be hard to understand at the outset, but it is a collection of writings that has lasted at least thirty-four-hundred years. This type of staying power adds to the relevance of its message. At its irreducible minimum, it is a set of fascinating stories that will entertain and challenge you, but I am convinced it is much more. The Bible is not the only source of truth;

there are many others and seeking out truth is a fascinating part of the journey of self-improvement.

Another method of planting good seed is through a practice of self-edification. We should affirm ourselves through words that plant and yield good thoughts. There are various books, courses, and websites dedicated to helping start a regimen of positive affirmations. But you can simply begin by telling yourself, 'I am unique, valuable, powerful, and capable of doing amazing things.' And then continue to build out your positive affirmations list by adding statements that affirm who you are. Repeat these statements on a daily basis, and before you know it, they will grow into actions that reflect their truth, fuel your momentum, and replenish your mindset.

Lastly, let me suggest a practice of prayer and meditation. The best time for us to implement this practice is at the beginning of our day. By doing so, we set a rhythm or foundation for our day, and the way we start something usually affects the way it ends. Personally, I begin my day with prayer and gratitude. There is much to be thankful for, and if we continually bring thankfulness to the forefront of our thoughts, it will help us cultivate and maintain a healthy mindset.

There is a well-known military tactic that states "The best defense is a good offense." Everything mentioned in this writing will help you create a good offensive strategy to defend against the war that rages in our minds, which, left unattended, defaults to chaos and negativity. Knowing this, we must engage daily in one of the most important battles of our life, the battle for our minds.

Strategy

> *"Strategy without tactics is the slowest route to victory. Tactics without strategy is the noise before defeat."* Sun Tzu

We must determine to fight only worthy opponents. Only after we have determined an opponent is worthy, we should then plan our strategy.

Aesop, the ancient Greek storyteller, left us with a story named "The Lion in Love." The story goes as follows:

A powerful lion was roaming about one day and saw a beautiful young lady. She was the daughter of a woodsman whose livelihood depended on his adeptness of the axe. As soon as the lion locked eyes with the beautiful young lady, his heart burned with passion and a desire to one day marry her. The lion approached the woodsman and asked for the young lady's hand in marriage. The woodsman, stricken with fear, knew that if he rejected the lion he was at risk of death. Instead of denying the lion's request, he conceded to his wishes on one condition. The lion would have to go to the nearby town and seek out a dentist and have his fangs removed, then return to the woodsman for inspection.

The lion did as the woodsman requested, and upon his return, the woodsman explained that the lion must do one more thing before he would allow the marriage. He told the lion to go back to town and find a tradesman who could remove his claws. The lion protested but his love for the woodsman's daughter was greater than his love of self, so he did as her father requested out of the joy he would gain once he returned clawless. The lion sought out a tradesman and had every claw removed, then returned to the woodsman with a joyful heart, looking forward to his promised marriage with the beautiful young lady.

After the woodsman confirmed the lion indeed had his fangs and claws removed, he took his trusty axe and bashed the lion's head in, rendering him lifeless and laid out before him and his daughter.[22]

There is a simple but important lesson to learn from this fable that was written over 2500 years ago. When we encounter an enemy, we must compare his strengths to ours, then use the strength that is in greatest proportion to our enemies, so that we have the greatest chance of defeating him. It is only by analysis that we can create a winning strategy.

A well-known fact of war is that battles are won in the general's tent but fought on the front lines. It is the strategy behind the fight that ultimately wins the war. Strategy and the tactics that flow from them are what defeat brute force time and time again.

One of the greatest stories of war tactics may be the story of the Greek's Trojan Horse used to overcome the fortified city of Troy. After a decade of war and failed attempts to infiltrate the city of Troy, the Greeks turned to subterfuge and strategy, instead of brute force. The story goes as follows:

> After ten years of attempted siege of the great city of Troy, the Greek warriors constructed a massive wooden horse and left it on the shore of Troy and then sailed away. Troy pulled the massive wooden structure into the city gates to put it on display as a war trophy symbolizing their triumph over their opponents.

> When the citizens of Troy fell fast asleep, the Greeks returned under cover of nightfall, and the men hidden inside the Trojan horse, who had now penetrated their enemy's compound, opened the gates of the city to allow the rest of their allied forces to enter the stronghold. The Greeks overtook Troy that night because they used a cunning strategy that played to the egos of their enemies.[23]

The next time we are faced with an enemy, we would be wise to remember the stories of The Lion in Love and The Trojan Horse. They remind us that when we come up against an enemy that can overpower us, we should survey our strengths and rely on a strategy to outwit our most powerful foes.

Fundamentalism

"A fundamentalist is a person who considers whether a fact is acceptable to his religion before he explores it." Seth Godin

Have you ever reflected on a period of your life and wondered, 'what was I thinking,' or 'how could I have been so different, off, or indifferent?' Have you ever passively assumed the thoughts and behaviors of people and influences around you? It is critical we ask these important questions of ourselves.

Our early years are formative—schooling, religion, friends, and family have a way of homogenizing us, coalescing our beliefs into a sort of groupthink. Powerful institutions and influences can have an effect on us that gradually paints our beliefs with broad strokes of similarity, and until we can regain the understanding that we were all born as individuals who have the power to think independently, we are at risk of delegating our most critical thinking to external sources.

I have written about the danger of groupthink or herd mentality. When I think of herd mentality, my mind immediately goes to Adolf Hitler and Nazi Germany. On November 21, 1922, the *New York Times* reported,

"Several reliable, well-informed sources confirmed the idea that Hitler's anti-Semitism was not so genuine or violent as it sounded, and that he was merely using anti-Semitic propaganda as a bait to catch masses of followers ...."[24]

In 1938, *Time* magazine named Adolf Hitler Man of the Year.[25] Slowly but surely, Hitler used institutions, religion, power structures, propaganda, German, and American media to program millions of people into believing it was not only acceptable but also a moral imperative to eradicate another human race. Hitler successfully indoctrinated a nation and turned his fellow countrymen into killing machines, but how did he do it? He methodically convinced millions to delegate their decision making to fundamentalist ideas.

There are many examples of this type of cult indoctrination throughout history, including the Branch Davidians of Waco, Texas, a religious sect led by David Koresh, who in 1993 was entangled in a fifty-one-day deadly standoff with the FBI. The showdown culminated in the death of seventy-six of Koresh's followers, including twenty-five children and two pregnant women. The Salem witch trials are yet another example of fundamentalism that grew to deadly force and claimed the lives of innocent people.

This extreme fundamentalism is not limited to America; there are countless examples throughout the world— 25,000 Feyli Kurds were killed in Iraq by Saddam

Hussein, the Rwanda genocide of an estimated 750,000 Tutsi people, and the 9/11 attacks on America. But the question still remains, 'why does this happen?'

Fundamentalism is often presented as an attempt to eradicate some evil, but its chief methods use some form, usually a guise, of evil to accomplish its task. Fundamentalism is often attributed to religion, but it also exists in corporate media, political ideology, many systems of education, corrupt governments such as Marxism and socialism, and a host of additional systems of thought that are at work programming their adopters.

Fundamentalism, essentially, offers to free its agents of the burden of thought, and in turn, it provides an operating system that guarantees a certain set of outcomes. If one buys into a system of fundamentals without critical analysis, he elects the belief system and its ramifications, usually disguised as rewards—such as ninety-nine virgins for the execution of infidels.

A fundamentalist is one who uses any system of thinking to accept or reject ideas without additional independent thinking. When the fundamentalist is faced with a question, he turns to his system for a decision instead of his ability to reason. Systems of thinking are both good and bad. They help us save time, make decisions on the fly, and keep us from distraction and danger, but if we are not careful, they can also severely blind us to the truth.

The fundamentalist uses powerful stories to hypnotize and blind followers who will listen. The stories typically use fear to motivate and maintain obedience; however, the stories begin with half-truths, just enough propaganda to plant a seed. The seed is then watered and reinforced for as long as it takes to grow into obedience in the follower. An additional cult follower is the most valuable win for the fundamentalist.

When we consume stories without a healthy dose of skepticism and analysis, we are at risk of blindly accepting the powerful narratives that are being fed to us. Narratives are active, there is a force inside them propagating them to the masses, and the only weapon we have to combat them is the power of our mind. An individual's ability to think is arguably the only sovereign power one has, but all too often, people give their only power away, delegating it to the storyteller—the fundamentalist narrator.

Now that we know the inherent dangers of fundamentalism and groupthink, how do we break free from it and begin to think for ourselves? The first thing we should do is 'allow' ourselves to question anything that smells of fundamentalism. We need to cultivate curiosity so that we can wrestle with and explore the ideas and stories that are being sent our way. But how do we do this?

Here are a few suggestions that will help you develop your autonomy: challenge your ideals, set aside critical thinking time, activate and develop your creativity.

Challenge Your Ideals

Make a list of five things you hold as very important and then challenge them. These ideas could be political or religious, beliefs about your health, they could even be about the relationships you maintain. Ask yourself why you hold each belief to be true. When you have the answer, question it too. Ask this question three levels deep. Below is an example of a question asked three levels deep.

Question:

Why is fundamentalism dangerous? Because it requires us to relinquish our decision-making power.

Why is giving our decision-making ability away a bad thing? Because it is the only sovereign control we have.

Why is giving our only sovereign control away a bad thing? Because we essentially hand over our future and accept responsibility for the outcomes.

Challenging our most deeply held ideas can be an eye-opening experience.

Set Aside Critical Thinking Time

The world has become a superfluous information economy. Most people think more information and experience is better, that it will lead to an expedited version of success, but information overload often eliminates our ability to think deeply.

Do you have time to think? When was the last time you sat and explored an idea for an hour? If your answers are 'no' and 'not sure' to the previous questions, you might consider setting aside some thinking time.

> *Emerson said, "The revelation of thought takes men out of servitude into freedom."*

Activate and Develop Your Creativity

This one may seem to be esoteric, but with a little discipline, it can be extremely rewarding and may be the most beneficial suggestion, long term. What creative exercise can you take up? Maybe it is dance or painting, or maybe it is coloring or woodworking?

There are limitless ways to be creative. I love to write because it allows me to create and think almost simultaneously, to dream while being awake, to explore the inner depths of my mind and soul. Zadie Smith wrote, "The very reason I write is so that I might not sleepwalk through my entire life."

Creativity questions everything and co-creates with the infinite.

Fundamentalism demands obedience from the finite. Beware of it; question everything. As we have seen, world wars, race eradications, polygamous cults, and jihadist attacks begin with "not so violent" (or so it was reported) propaganda, just enough bait to catch the masses.

Influence

---

*"When all is said and done, more will
be said than done." Aesop*

The definitions surrounding the idea of influence are
pervasive; we hear things like, 'people don't care how
much you know until they know how much you care,'
and 'leadership is influence,' and 'influence is the ability
to get others to do what we do not want to do.' There are
entire books written about influence, but the power and
the ability to wield it is still mysterious in many respects.

A friend of mine once said, 'our influence is never
neutral—it is either positive or negative.' Our influence
is either dragging people down or pushing them forward.
I agree with this idea of influence ... on the contrary, a
static influence is an oxymoron, a misnomer of sorts. My
concern in this writing is to explore the positive
influence that one can have in the lives of others. But
what exactly is personal influence in the purest and most
positive form? We need to understand this because
influence is valuable and powerful, so powerful that
cultures rise and fall because of it.

Influence can be intoxicating and can lead to
corruption—see Lucifer, Hitler, some politicians, and
fear-based, agenda-driven media. These sources of

negative influence knowingly use propaganda to manipulate and prey on the emotions of others. These sources of negative influence always lead their followers toward chaos and destruction but are not the focus of this writing.

Influence, in my estimation, is an undefinable pull, a type of magnetic attraction on others that persuades them in the direction of a leader or influencer. Influence is an effect, a persuasion of values or ambition that another person desires to experience and sometimes adopts as their own. Influence elicits a change in action or thinking from the people it touches. Positive influence calls others to proactivity—to evolve one's thinking and methods, to help them create a better future, so we can say that influence in its purest form is life giving.

Action is a precedent of influence. The great influencers of history never said, 'Go march for a cause, here is a map,' they said, 'I am marching for a cause, join me!' The former example does not work, the latter sets a precedent of action. There is always an energy about influence, so I will attempt to explain a few action precedents that ultimately lead to influence, the first being giving, the second being vision casting, and the third being moral transcendence.

Giving
An influencer who gives of their time, experience, or finances simultaneously creates a sense of obligation in the one being given to. Influencers, at least the types we

are dealing with here, do not give for the sake of reciprocity; nonetheless, reciprocation is a natural byproduct of giving. Take for example a compliment. If someone compliments a person on their personality, a physical characteristic, or an action they perform, the receiver of said compliment is obliged to an in-kind response, a thank you or some other form of gratitude. The response to an influencer's giving is usually met with a varying degree of proportional reciprocation.

The influence that giving carries with it is often used as a less benevolent tool. To explore this concept in action, one only needs to give a little attention to politics. Campaign contributions often weigh heavily on the decisions made by politicians and oftentimes lead to quid pro quo behavior.

Vision Casting

Casting a grand vision is another method of influence. There is an attraction to grand visions that stand out and capture the attention of others. Where all else is constant and there is no vision, there is less energy among any group of people. We as humans were given the ability to dream for a reason; that reason is to help bring ideas that were once thought impossible to life. This type of vision casting has powerful effects.

In 2004, Peter Diamandis created a grand vision that aroused the world. He established the XPRIZE, a competition that in theory would award a $10 million cash prize to the team that could develop a private spaceship. At the time of the XPRIZE announcement, Peter only had a vision of what could be, but because of his grand vision, he was able to inspire the world. After hearing about Peter's grand vision, a wealthy benefactor stepped up and provided the prize money, the missing piece of the puzzle, the prize in the XPRIZE. Next, teams from around the world began attempting to build private spacecrafts to compete for the prize money.

The inaugural XPRIZE was awarded to Mojave Aerospace Ventures. Since winning, the company has gone on to license their award-winning spacecraft to Virgin Galactic. For just over $250,000 you can reserve a seat on one of Virgin Galactic's private space flights. A multi-billion-dollar private space industry now exists. This incredible reality was influenced by a grand vision.

The third action of influence is performed through moral transcendence. This idea is a bit more abstract than the previous two, so I encourage you to try and remove any preconceptions before reading any further.

Moral Transcendence
Moral transcendence has the power to influence others. When I refer to morals, I mean to write about the system of ethics we ascribe to and the values those beliefs produce that influence our behavior. When I write about transcendence, I mean to write about the act of surpassing our current state of morality, or ethical behavior. This moral transcendence, then, is working to surpass our current state of 'goodness' through certain

actions. The more we work to morally transcend, the more we become other minded. We begin to think about how we can release kindness into the world around us and impact the human race for the better.

The action of moral transcendence is limitless, meaning we can never fully transcend ourselves morally, but we can strive to show more kindness, empathy, and respect for others. When we act on this belief, we will begin to change the world, one action at a time. When we help those in need, we transcend the default human state, egocentrism. When others witness this transcendence, they cannot help but take notice of the phenomenon. Please do not confuse what I am suggesting; by no means am I referring to piety, any form of religious dogmatism, or self-righteousness.

The ideas and the actions of moral transcendence are very powerful because they are inclusive of giving and vision casting, the other two forms of influence. Through moral transcendence, we show others a grander vision of humanity while giving of ourselves. If you are curious about how moral transcendence looks in practice, I encourage you to research the lives of Martin Luther King Jr., Harriet Tubman, and William Wilberforce.

The famous storyteller, Aesop, left the world with a clue to influence when he wrote, "When all is said and done, more will be said than done."

People of influence, like the ones listed above, are people of action who understand just how powerful one person's influence can be. They are people who give, cast grand visions, and strive for moral transcendence.

More

> *"If I wanted to destroy a nation, I would give it too much, and I would have it on its knees, miserable, greedy, sick." John Steinbeck*

'More' is oftentimes a very dangerous idea. I used to be a huge believer in the power of more. Today we hear people talk about what they need to be happy or successful, and invariably it has to do with needing just a little bit more. More takes on different faces such as: money, possessions, or power, but 'more' is always just out of reach.

It is easy to fall into the trap of thinking we need just a little bit of something we don't have before we can be happy. The desire for more is born from deep cultural programming that stems from a society that is obsessed with excess. The problem with more is that it has no destination, even the word itself is unending, similar to the disease it creates inside of us. It's impossible to arrive at 'more.' Instead, the ravenous mindset continues to consume the life it infects.

Today, our calendars, pantries, garages, luxury car collections, and mental capacities are overflowing with excess. We are in danger of becoming gluttons who believe one more bite is all we need to be satisfied, when in fact what we 'need' is far less, a steady diet of decluttering. The average person's needs are being held hostage and extorted by their desires. What we truly need is an elimination diet from things, the time consumers, the next best toys, and the marketing messages that constantly hypnotize and program our appetites for excess.

The goal should be to become rich in life, life itself, not things, and I believe this can be accomplished with a simple—though not easy—mindset shift. When we create space for what is most important, only then can we cherish the things that bring true joy in our lives. The question becomes 'what brings true joy in life?' This is a question we should ask and revisit often. The earlier and more frequently we ask ourselves this question, the better off our lives will be.

When we have identified what is truly important to us, we can then work to make it the foundation of our joy. After surveying what is truly important, most will have concluded money and possessions are not high on the list. We can begin to make room in our life for that which is most important by reprioritizing. The method of doing this is also countercultural.

We must first begin to rid our lives of the weight of possessions and their dizzying pursuits. Once we do this it becomes clearer that a peaceful 'enough' is far greater than an unquenchable desire for 'more.'

If this idea seems simple, that's because it is, but simple is not always easy, especially when consumerism has been programmed into a society like ours. We were designed to enjoy life in meaningful relationships—hoarding and ultra-consumption is against our nature. If you are having trouble accepting this idea, allow me to point you to the words of those who swam in excess for decades.

W.H. Vanderbilt said, "The care of $200 million is enough to kill anyone. There is no pleasure in it." Henry Ford said, "I was happier when doing a mechanic's job." John D. Rockefeller said, "I have made many millions, but they have brought me no happiness." Andrew Carnegie said, "Millionaires seldom smile." John Steinbeck, Pulitzer Prize winning author wrote, "If I wanted to destroy a nation, I would give it too much, and I would have it on its knees, miserable, greedy, sick."[26]

What are you striving for? Is it room for what is most important? Or is it the trap of more?

Busyness

"Beware the barrenness of a busy life." Socrates

Sometimes I feel as though this hustle culture has gotten the best of me and most of those around me, as though I am drowning in the details of a thousand unfinished projects. These projects multiply into a frenzy of disconnectedness, sometimes keeping me from that which is most important. At times I have felt a mile wide but only inches deep, spread thin—merely a film that reaches to touch as much as possible.

I am guilty of going too fast, of robbing myself and those around me of the attention they need and deserve. I am guilty of looking at the days as check-off lists and saying, 'If I can just stack up a bunch of days and fill them with as many things as possible, somehow I will achieve progress.'

At times I've treated people like tasks that crowd out my agenda. I have starved myself of the details of life, nuance, multicolor, and simplicity. I have missed 'connection' because I was thinking about the next month, year, and decade. I have come to find out I am only guaranteed now. I am guilty of being greedy and trying to take the future in my hands, which can never be done, while allowing the present to slip through them.

I've traded the present for daydreams of grandeur and wantonness, and who knows how many years I have lost. But today it stops, and I slow. Today I begin to focus on the now—to keep it from blurring into a decade of displaced desire and worry.

I will notice the colors in the sunlight and the trees as they dance about, carried by the strength of the invisible wind. I will admire how the mist falls when it begins to rain—how it coats the blades of grass that reach for the cloud-blanketed sky. I will not forget to look at the intricate design of the cardinal on my fence and notice how the black and red weave together in its coat of color. I will listen to the words and notes of each song and pay them their due.

Most importantly, today, I will make time for others because they deserve it, and crave it, and I can help them—just as they can help me. Together, we will notice the beauty of today with all of its power, splendor, and wonder. When someone asks for my attention, I will notice the gift they carry along with them, the one I have overlooked and discounted for far too long, their gift of relationship—the only thing that truly matters in life.

Enough with the shackles of appointments, notifications and calendar slots. I'll trade them in for conversations, hugs, heart-to-hearts, and face-to-face connections. I will make connections with humans who matter and care not about what's next ... but about what's now.

Focus

"Simplicity is the ultimate sophistication." Socrates

It is true that a concentrated drip of water, if constant over time, has the power to drill through rock. This is the power of continued focus—it can penetrate the strongest of barriers. Focus uses the power of concentrated energy to create wonderment. It comes to the aid of the PhD student, it steadies the hand of the surgeon, and it harnesses the power of the limitless mind.

When there is a lack of focus the mind is sent spinning like a reckless pinball bouncing from bumper to bumper, usually ending up in a gutter. Sometimes lack of focus entertains us, but it distracts us from our mission. It leaves us tired, confused, and restless.

Steven Pressfield, in his magnum opus, *The War of Art*, tells us the lack of focus, or what he calls Resistance, is what keeps us from our purpose. He says that Resistance is somewhat of a shape shifter—that it comes in many forms. It can disguise itself as a noble venture, an educational pursuit, a glass of wine, or anything else that pulls us from what we know we should be doing.[27]

To name something is powerful—we can call this force, the one that keeps us from our purpose, Resistance, evil, sin, the great oppressor, or anything else we would like to. The benefit to naming it is we can then see it for what it is, track it down, and fight it. I battle against this force daily. Most of my Resistance shows up as fear or unworthiness.

My Resistance questions: 'Who are you to be a writer?' And, 'Shouldn't you get a real job?'

For years my focus was inhibited by not believing I had something valuable to say, but this was a lie, a false narrative played and bought into time and time again. The thing about our thoughts, and this is very important, is they are a self-fulfilling prophecy, seeds of our action and future. The good news is—we have the ability to control our thoughts.

Many people allow the demands and expectations of others to drown out their focus. They are directed by the loud voices from their parents, bosses, coworkers, best friends, the news, and the list goes on ad infinitum, and if I can assure you of one thing, let it be this: if you do not choose your future, someone else will choose it for you.

Herbert Bayard Swope, three-time Pulitzer Prize-winning journalist said, "I can't give you a surefire formula for success, but I can give you a formula for failure: try to please everybody all the time."

Those who understand focus and leverage are happy to harness your energy, talents, and time, then focus it on their agenda. Beware of this, but don't take this the wrong way. We should find a way to serve others, but invariably, the best way to serve others is through our masterpiece work, the work only we can do because of the talents we have been given to serve with. Focusing our energy, time, and talent on a noble calling is the most efficient path to doing great work while serving others.

According to one of the most cited and divisive studies[28] on the human attention span, conducted by Microsoft, the human attention span has dropped from twelve seconds in the year 2000 to eight seconds in 2013. The most surprising statistic in the research is the stated attention span of the average goldfish, which is recorded at a second longer than humans, at nine seconds. This research has been refuted but mainly by opinion and proponents of mythical multitasking.

Since this writing is about focus, let's get back to it. With the overwhelming research about how our attention span is dwindling, is there anything we can do to combat the phenomenon? The answer is yes, but it takes discipline. Here are a few ways to win back your ability to focus through discipline.

Start by committing to doing really hard things. Consider starting or finishing a degree or some other educational venture. Education is a great investment that will pay dividends, and it is a hard thing to do because it requires time, focus, and other scarce resources to follow through with.

Benjamin Franklin said, "An investment in knowledge pays the best interest."

Cal Newport wrote *Deep Work*, a book about the importance and rising value for work that is performed under intense focus. Newport's definition of deep work is as follows: "Professional activities performed in a state of distraction-free concentration that push your cognitive capabilities to their limit."[29]

Newport argues that as humans' ability to focus decreases on a macro level, the demand for focused, *Deep Work*, increases in value. One of his recommendations is something I have done for years now to enable deep work; that is time blocking.

Time blocking is simple. Use your schedule to block out times for specific work or tasks you need to accomplish. Use time intervals that are achievable for you. I use one-hour blocks of time, and I allow myself at least ten minutes as a break at the top of each hour. Time blocking allows you to set aside planned blocks of productivity that can aid you in your endeavors to perform focused deep work.

Using a daily task list that includes a rank order priority will help you focus on what's most important. I sit down every day and write out my seven tasks for the day, if I have not already done it the night before. Next, I list a number beside each task, one being the most important and seven being the least important. The first tasks are usually the ones that are hardest, least fun, and require the most intense focus.

Throughout the day, the mind tires and we gradually lose our ability to intentionally focus, so placing the most critical tasks at the start of the day ensures they get an adequate amount of attention.

Focus is now a quasi-superpower because of the proliferation of distractions: dings, inbox chimes, social media bells, and all of the other notifications vying for a share of our attention, an attempt to direct our time and talent toward the desires of others.

But, if we are to fulfill our desires and callings, it will be done by way of our time and talents ushered in by a good understanding of the power and scarcity of focus. If we can harness the power of focus, it will aid us in giving the best we have to offer.

Connection

> *"You know the problem with the rat race is, even if you win, you're still a rat." Lily Tomlin*

The Amish people are really interesting, are they not? Some might suggest they have life figured out while others might say they are just different. One thing I cannot argue is the Amish have some advantages over the thinly spread, washed up, hung out to dry, rat race cultures that abound today.

I once heard a joke by Lily Tomlin, and it has stuck with me like a mind splinter ever since. She said: "You know the problem with the rat race is, even if you win, you're still a rat."

I heard the joke at the so called 'height of my career.' It was the first time I had ever felt a little ... rat-like. Day after day, the race consumed me while I chased my next block of cheese—at that time my cheese took forms like the next raise, next client, next promotion—all so that I could attain just a little more success because, at the time, that is what I thought life was about. I began to survey my life and wonder if there wasn't a better way, a more fulfilling way to live.

I came to the conclusion that my life had no meaningful connections with others because I had left them all in the dust, racing toward my next goal. I had bounced from one goal to another, stacking up milestones of success, and even when spending time with others, I was thinking about my agenda. I was never present; instead, I was off in the future planning my worldwide cheese domination. What a way to live—gliding through life on a sled of egocentrism, demanding all that it could offer.

While attending a business event, I heard the now former manager of the Houston Astros, A.J. Hinch, speak on why his team was so successful. It was a few months after they'd won the National Championship in 2017. He explained that their winning strategy was in the 'connections' he helped establish and nurture between his team's players.

He went on to explain that he helped create meaningful connections between his players by assigning his senior players tasks that helped facilitate connections with his junior players. The assignments took time, care, and money out of his player's pockets to accomplish.

Hinch gave an example of the simplicity behind his strategy of creating connection: he once made Justin Verlander buy a surfboard for one of his rookie teammates and then teach him how to surf. The two teammates formed a relationship that made the team stronger. Hinch assigned these 'connection tasks' between players throughout the team, in turn creating a strong fabric of relationships between all the members.

But why? Why is connection so fundamental to high functioning groups of people?

The United States Military may be one of the largest and most successful organizations at facilitating connections among high-functioning groups of people. In the military, men and women are grouped into fireteams, small units of three to five that are oftentimes responsible for each other's lives. This creates deep connections—bonds hard to break between fireteam members. These connections often outlast military careers and span the entire lives of the team members.

The deep meaningful connections made in small groups, often called tribes, are what seem to interlock human souls. I still keep up with two men I deployed with to Iraq. During our times of fear, stupidity, and connectedness, something happened. Our relationships were forged into more than friendships, meaningful connections that resonated deep into our identity.

Throughout my twenties and early thirties, I didn't understand the importance of connection, but now I cherish it. As life motors on down the road, the allure of status and possessions seems to fade away, and the basic need for connection increases evermore. The novelty of things becomes more and more trivial, and time becomes a great teacher by continually clarifying priorities.

Meaningful connections are the infrastructure for relationships and all meaningful things that flow from them. The stronger the connection, the stronger the foundation for everything that is built on top of it. The Amish, the Astros, and the U.S. Military all have something they share in common which makes them great. What makes them world-class, are the deep connections that exist between their people.

The path to anything great and lasting—business, marriage, legacy, and influence—will always come through deep, meaningful connections.

Time Travel

*"The whole future lies in uncertainty:
live immediately." Seneca*

On October 28th, 2013, I stopped digging. The saying, 'you hit rock bottom when you stop digging,' finally made sense for me, and I laid down my shovel. The very next day I attended my first Alcoholics Anonymous meeting and met some unlikely friends who taught me invaluable life lessons every time we got together. Eventually, I found a sponsor who helped guide me through the early days of recovery. I would call him when the anger, restlessness, and discontent set in, when I needed to vent and glean advice from someone who had walked in my shoes and had a few more sobriety birthdays under his belt.

Most often, my calls were made to complain about how others, a boss, coworker, or complete stranger, had wronged me. I would call and explain how my past or present had not given me what I believed I deserved (the sheer amount of 'I's in my complaints should have been a sign of who the real problem was—'twas I). One of the realizations that came too many years later was—my tendency to judge the actions of others in an attempt to prop myself up. It was prideful self-righteousness at its worst. I finally discovered the self-righteous are always tenants of victimhood.

One of my sponsor's favorite sayings was, 'Terry, get out of your time machine.'

I often remind myself to get and stay out of my time machine. Let me explain. I used to struggle with life—mainly my past—so in an attempt to get over issues, I would travel back to various arguments, situations in which I thought I was wronged, and other injustices to grapple with them. I would make judgments to settle the matters, rendering one-sided verdicts for all from a solitary judge, jury, and executioner—me.

When I was not time-traveling into the past, I'd find myself time-traveling thirty years into the future sorting out all that I would need to be happy. It went something like this: 'Before I can retire and truly live, I will need a couple million in the bank, a great sports car, a big house, an even bigger vacation house, a boat …' the list went on.

Don't take this the wrong way. I have no problem with dreaming a little, in fact, I encourage it; I still do it sometimes, but the crux of the matter for me came when I realized I was spending too much time dreaming up my ideal future while robbing my present and everyone around me, a sort of psychological socialism. Robbing Peter to pay Paul is never fair to Peter or his family. The time I spent dreaming about all I needed before I could be happy was a form of escapism. It kept me from appreciating the moment, all we really have.

My sponsor's reminders still echo in my mind today and serve as pillars of wisdom. 'Terry, get out of your time machine,' these simple words, saved me from much heartache.

Over the past few years, I have done my very best to metaphorically permanently disable my time machine. Every now and then the motherboard fires back up; the engine begins to smoke, chug, and clank. Familiar noises from my once-trusty time machine entice me for another trip into the past or future, but I know better. So, I head on out to the junkyard, where I store the time machine, and snip a few more wires to further render it useless.

I have become keenly aware the less time I spend in the past or future, the more I am able to spend in the joy of today.

Do you have a time machine, and if so, how much time do you spend time-traveling in it? I hope this writing encourages you to park it and get back to living.

"This only is denied, even to God: the
power to undo the past."
Agathon

Company

---

*"The unexamined life is not worth
living."*
Socrates

The company we keep will ultimately determine the quality of our life. I have heard it said that we will be an average of our five closest friends. If this is true, we should be mindful of those we allow into our lives.

People travel about their day with energy. I am referring to the energy of the spirit and personality that is emitted from each of us. Whether we know it or not, we are sending energy out into the lives of others. Our energy will either lift others or pull them down. Sometimes this energy is so subtle, it can go unnoticed for quite some time. Other times we take notice of one's energy before they ever say a word. It comes across in their eyes, their posture, the creases in their face, and the distance between their footsteps.

I was once accused of walking like I was on a mission. My boss told me that my walk was intimidating, that my pace was too fierce. It was a reflection of my energy, of what was happening on the inside, and for the setting I was working in, it needed to be shifted into a lower gear.

Have you ever spent time around someone whose energy was negative? Usually, a strong negative energy can be spotted easily when a person walks into the room or engages in a conversation. Their tone of voice is sad or aggressive, their shoulders are slightly tilted forward, their foreheads wrinkled, and faces grimaced. Their energy fills the room with a grey film of heaviness. Can you picture this person in your mind's eye? Can you name someone in your life who fits this description?

What about the opposite? Is there someone in your life who always carries a proverbial ray of sunshine in their back pocket? When they enter the room, their face fills with a smile, a seemingly contagious one that leaps to your face. Their voice carries a tone of excitement, a zeal that is electric. This person identifies a positive strain in most every situation because they intentionally seek it out. Even when they lose, they win, because they learn a valuable lesson in doing so. This type of person raises the energy level around them, and their force is so positive, it has the power to lift the spirits of others. They are determined to be undeterred.

We may need to survey the people closest to us—it's a simple exercise. Take out a sheet of paper and draw a cross on it. Write a simple description of both types of people mentioned in this writing, positive and negative. Then, think of the ten closest people in your life, the people you interact with most, and list them on either side of the cross you have drawn under the category they fall into. The last step is to take a deep, long, self-examining look into your behaviors and answer the question, 'Which side do I belong on?'

This is a tough but revealing exercise. Are you a negative person who emits an energy that drags others down? Or, are you the type of person who uses their energy to encourage, lift, and inspire others?

Pay close attention to this idea from Ralph Waldo Emerson:

> *"People do not seem to realize that*
> *their opinion of the world is also a*
> *confession of character."*

This quote from Emerson can be cutting, almost offensive, depending on where you find yourself at the time of its reading. If you have honestly answered the questions above and labeled yourself as one who struggles with negativity, this idea may even be dreadful, but there is hope. Adjusting our paradigm, our outlook on life, is not only possible, but it is also a worthy challenge.

If one identifies as being a negative person, he has a choice. He can move himself to the right side of the chart (the positive side) and eventually take others with him or continue to pull others into negativity. The choice is each of ours to make.

If we discover we are already putting off positive energy, we need to do what we can to continue to draw people to our side of thinking and realize that if we have too many negative influences in our life, eventually, they will take a toll on us. Let this serve as a reminder for us to keep watch over the company we keep. We need a tribe, a band of brothers or sisters, that spurs us along in a positive direction, not a group of naysayers who infect our lives with negativity.

The poet philosopher, David Whyte, wisely cautions,

> *"Sometimes it takes darkness and the*
> *sweet confinement of your aloneness*
> *to learn anything or anyone that does*
> *not bring you alive is too small*
> *for you."*

Communication

---

*"When there is a lack of
communication, people go negative."*
Jon Gordon

This idea may be the most valuable piece of information you get from this book. It was for me when I read it in a Jon Gordon book years ago. "When there is a void in communication, negativity will fill it."[30]

Unfortunately, we as humans naturally default to negativity when there is a void in communication. And because communication is the bedrock on which relationships are built and sustained, without it, they slowly disintegrate.

My friends and family are strewn across the United States, many in different time zones. It is easy to go months without talking to some of them, and admittedly my thinking defaults to, 'there must be a problem,' or 'they must not want to speak to me.' There is some faint trace of unjustified abandonment in my thinking when there is a lack of communication for some time. Despite there being no evidence, even the slightest minutia of proof, that our relationship has suffered, as sure as the sun sets—a wedge begins to settle in when there is a void in communication.

Stephen Covey wrote, "That which is most personal, is most general." The idea suggests that if one of us struggles with something deeply personal, there is a high probability that many suffer from the same personal issue, and that it may be a part of the general human condition. No doubt this 'feeling,' which comes upon us due to a lack in communication, is some sort of a low-grade separation anxiety stemming from a lack of meaningful connection.

Early in human history, our ancestors lived communally, in a high-touch environment. They communicated in person, face-to-face, to survive, and it became their relational glue. This type of connection is no longer necessary for survival and has all but vanished; however, instinctually, it seems that we miss it, even need it on some deep humanistic level.

The truth is if communication is lacking, relationships are at risk. Since relationships are and always have been the most important aspect in life, communication is arguably one of the most important functions we can perform. The importance of continually communicating with those we care about cannot be overstated. So, when there is a void in communication, we have at our disposal the ability to insert assurance of our care through simple conversation, which has a way of adding life back into a fading relationship.

This can be a challenge for many because of the pace of life—today we are connected, superficially at least, with a great number of people, but we must remind ourselves how vital relationships are so we can prioritize our lives accordingly.

When we reach out to someone and communicate with them, it reminds them of their importance to us at least. One of the greatest gifts we can give to another person is our attention and time, two of the scarcest resources we have. If we discover that we cannot find the time to communicate with those who are important to us, it may be time to rid our lives of less important things. It is easy to be swept away by the trivial—at the expense of what is most important, our family, friends, and colleagues.

Remember that if we are failing to communicate with others, they may be wondering why we do not care about them, because when there is a lack of communication, people almost always default to negativity. Communication is vital. It keeps us from isolating and bonds relationships—the most important aspect of life—tightly together.

Superpower

"If you speak when angry, you'll make the best speech you'll ever regret." Groucho Marx

My youngest son, Liam, allows himself to get so worked up at times, as do I along with most other emotional beings. Fortunately, I have graduated from collapsing to the floor, but I still crumble on the inside and lose my temper far too often.

One day my son got so angry, he collapsed to the floor and began yelling that everyone was against him and life was unfair. My response to my son was, 'Son, you know, you have a superpower if you will just use it, that power is staying calm.' Admittedly, this is much easier said than done.

I believe we all have access to this superpower and if we will use it, it can help us create a gap between what happens to us (stimulus) and how we react to what happens to us (our response). I first learned about this concept from Viktor Frankl's book, *A Man's Search for Meaning*. It has been repeated many times, in many books, but it is so important, it bears repeating. Frankl taught, "Between stimulus and response there is a space.

In that space is our power to choose our response. In our response lies our growth and our freedom."[31]

To add to this concept, let me include an idea from the late comedian Groucho Marx who once remarked, "If you speak when angry, you'll make the best speech you'll ever regret."

When we are instigated by any type of harmful stimulus, something that arouses negative emotions in us, through discipline we can build a habit of adding calmness and time before we respond. A superpower, in my estimation, is a rare use of skill or behavior only seen in extremely wise or mighty beings; this idea of adding calm and time to a divisive situation certainly qualifies as one.

Take for example the wisdom of the ancient proverb, "Even a fool who keeps silent is considered wise; when he closes his lips, he is deemed intelligent."[32]

This superpower is available to everyone, but very few will use it.

Wisdom

---

*"Every man I meet is my superior in
some way. In that, I learn of him."*
Ralph Waldo Emerson

When I think back to my twenties, I realize just how foolish I was. Today, I am often impressed with the younger generation. They seem much wiser than I was at their age, and this is a great thing. At some point in life many people realize a switch has been flipped. Some call it the *eureka* moment or the *light bulb* moment, and no matter what we call it, the moment happens when we realize we have much left to learn; it is at this point that our paradigm shifts to a learning mindset.

This is a watershed moment in life. Judgements begin to fade away, curiosity courses through us, and we take an interest in other points of view, our mind is opened to the great breadth of information that exists. We gain a new appreciation for debate, and the things that once challenged us seem to be useful tools for growth. I encourage everyone to get to this point in their life as quickly as possible. When we see ourselves as students, our lives begin to open up to many new possibilities. Until we begin looking for teachers of various forms, we remain in neutral as life speeds forward.

As the ancient proverb states, "When the student is ready, the teacher will appear."

It is true that when someone is ready to learn, there is a fresh beginning, a new chapter in their life. When the student is ready, everything in life becomes her teacher. When a student is ready, they shift their eyes from the little they know to the vast learnings that are omnipresent.

Emerson said, "Every man I meet is my superior in some way. In that, I learn of him."

When we begin to seek wisdom, we can find it in limitless sources around us. We should seek wisdom as if it were gold, become prospectors for nuggets of wisdom. We can think of ourselves as limitless vessels and attempt to fill ourselves with as much wisdom as possible.

A helpful analogy is to think of a river. Let's use the mighty Colorado River as an example. Imagine a tiny straw. If you were to throw a straw into the great power of the Colorado, it would be tossed to and fro, slammed against the rocks by the rapids repeatedly until it finally washed up on the riverbank somewhere. But even the tiniest of straws, if positioned just right in the mightiest of rivers, will act as a flow through for the current.

Similarly, if we position ourselves just right in any situation, we can learn from the flow of wisdom that proceeds from it, but before this can happen, we must make the choice to become a student. I consider myself a prospector of wisdom and make it a point to (metaphorically) put on my headlamp and grab my pickaxe every morning. I prepare myself mentally to be on the lookout for nuggets of wisdom throughout the day. When I find one, I tuck it away for future reference.

Over the past few years I have kept a running document with nuggets of wisdom, little pieces of advice from various sources. It has developed into a twenty-page document that I review at least a few times a week. It acts as a guide—keeping me on a path of learning. I attribute much happiness and success to this list of wisdom I have been compiling and recommend that everyone makes it a habit to wake up daily and don their (metaphorical) prospector gear; then, throughout the day, keep your eyes open for nuggets of wisdom to store away for future review.

A great place to search for these nuggets of wisdom is our past. We can dig through our past experience and begin to pull out pieces of wisdom, which we should have learned from, to make sure they do not fade away in vain.

Books that have lasted decades and sometimes centuries are another good source of wisdom. They are still around because they have been vetted by others. They compete with novel books because they have proven their worth, and they are rife with wisdom, but we must mine them and look for it.

Finally, mentors and coaches are great sources of wisdom. People who have experienced life, gone before us, made mistakes, and accomplished great things can save us much time and heartache if we will ask them for their guidance. Most people will help us if we will lay down our pride and just ask for it.

When we intentionally look for sources of wisdom, they will appear as naturally as the morning sun.

Responsibility

---

*"The price of greatness is
responsibility." Winston Churchill*

If not me, who? This can be one of the scariest and most rewarding questions to ask and answer. I often wonder if some of the great people of world history such as Harriet Tubman, Nelson Mandela, and Corrie ten Boom asked themselves the same question, 'If not me, who?'

Responsibility is a fascinating and complex idea worthy of our interest and debt. It drives some to spend their entire lives on a single cause and allows others to demand from life all that it can give while floating on a sea of expectations and entitlements. The problem, mystery, and sometimes brilliance of responsibility is that it is subjective. We cannot change a person's responsibility, just as we cannot shift the direction of the wind. We can only respond to our convictions, ideals, and high callings.

When there is a widespread lack of responsibility, destruction ensues, idle hands go to work chipping away at the very structures that uphold their privilege—tearing down the barriers that protect the values they molest. G.K. Chesterton said, "Don't ever take a fence down until you know the reason it was put up."

People who lack values tear down instead of building up. Their ignorance of responsibility destroys people and ideas, and if allowed to run rampant, can ultimately tear down entire nations. One only needs to reference the history of Nazi Germany to see what a one-time rogue sect of irresponsible people can destroy if left undeterred for too long.

Symbols such as the American flag, presidential monuments, and war memorials reinforce the ideals our country was built upon. They were built in memorial to great sacrifices that were paid. When symbols are attacked, the ideas of what they once stood for is destroyed along with them, but why? Hate-bred destruction only creates dissension and erosion—it never leads to preservation or greatness.

If you are an American, by birth or immigration, you enjoy some of the richest freedoms any group of people has ever experienced, but they are being attacked and are at risk. These freedoms and the symbols that represent them have been and will always be a part of a larger war between good and evil. Too often, people enjoy the benefits of freedom without realizing the price that was paid for them.

I stumbled upon the idea of freedom and responsibility being inextricably linked when I read these words from Viktor Frankl:

"Freedom is in danger of degenerating into mere arbitrariness unless it is lived in terms of responsibleness. That is why I recommend that the Statue of Liberty on the East Coast be supplemented by a Statue of Responsibility on the West Coast."[33]

If you are one of the most fortunate people to walk the earth, one who has never lacked the great gift of freedom, let me elaborate on its importance with a personal story. It wasn't until I was without freedom, that I truly began to understand what it was worth. In 2003, I found myself at the end of a deployment in Iraq. At the time I had spent the better part of seven months participating in a war now known as Operation Iraqi Freedom.

After a trip to the post exchange (the base store), I glanced at my bank account balance after purchasing some essentials to get me through my week. I had saved close to $15,000 over the deployment, and I distinctly remember saying to myself, 'I would trade every dollar in my bank account for one day of freedom back home in America.' This was no statement made in haste; it was a trade I was willing to make on the spot for one day of freedom because I had finally learned its true value.

It is amazing how much we value things when we no longer have them. If you agree with this idea, that our freedom is near priceless, let me suggest that we have a personal responsibility to uphold that very freedom. We should guard it by honoring the sacrifices and protecting the institutions that helped create it. We should cherish it by respecting the blood sacrifices that bought our freedom. We should respect the symbols that memorialize our ancestors who fought and died for our freedom, always preserving its foundations.

But how can individuals be responsible for something as pervasive and, at times, as nebulous as freedom? How do those who are born into freedom—like many people are, never having paid for it—appreciate and value the gift that it is? We as a people are at risk of creating an entitled generation—a class of people who expect something as great as freedom at no cost to themselves. Freedom without a cost or a sense of responsibility owed to it will lead to an impoverished nation, a people that lack character and values. This is an issue we must broach. We can do this in many ways, but I have listed a few below as suggested starting points.

The first thing every person who benefits from the amazing gift of freedom should do is try to understand it. Study it, celebrate it, and most importantly, honor the freedoms you experience. We have a responsibility, I believe, to not only uphold this amazing gift of freedom but also to make it better, by sharing it with others. When we share something, it is extended and multiplied beyond us.

Next, we should do everything within our power to pass on the skills, experience, and gifts we have attained in our life to those who are less fortunate. If you are a writer, teacher, businesswoman, college graduate, medical doctor, or landscape architect, there is a generation of people coming up behind you that needs your expertise. You have achieved something amazing in your life—in part—because of the systems built on a foundation of freedom; now it is time to help others achieve their dreams and realize the value of freedom for themselves.

Lastly, whatever you decided to do, do it now. Don't wait for the perfect time. There is someone who desperately needs your help. We have the ability to alter a life through our encouragement and influence. Let's realize the awesome freedom we have and take the responsibility of passing its power onto others. Benjamin Disraeli understood responsibility when he said,

> *"The greatest good you can do for another is not just to share your riches but to reveal to him his own."*

Freedom and responsibility should go hand in hand; they are great riches we should cherish and do our best to pass on.

Service

*"Service to others is the rent we pay
for the privilege of living on earth."*
N. Eldon Tanner

I remember a lot of stories from my time in the military, but there is one that stands out most. It was just after we entered Iraq in March of 2003. I was a part of the initial ground forces that breached the massive sand berms that separate Northern Kuwait from Southern Iraq.

A day or two into our travel from Kuwait toward Baghdad, our hundred-vehicle convoy stopped on the side of the road for some unknown reason. It was a quintessential 'hurry up and wait moment' the U.S. military is known for, except this one would be much longer.

We were informed we were to build a temporary camp and wait for further orders. The pit stop turned into a four-day layover. About halfway through the stay my friend, HM3 Rezek, approached me and said, 'Hey Weaver, let's take the ambulance, sneak away, and go help some of the local Iraqi people who are in dire need of medical attention.'

Just before we, the U.S. Marines and a few Navy corpsmen entered the country, the Air Force ripped through the country and bombed hundreds of military compounds and state buildings over the course of six days and nights, better known as the 'shock and awe campaign.' The Iraqi people were in disarray, and many were without medical attention because most of the medical professionals, those who had money, fled the country leading up to the war.

Still, I was shocked by my friend Rezek's idea, so I inquired, 'You want to leave all the Marines, who have all the big guns [we carried pistols], and go help the people who are technically our enemies?'

His only reply was, 'Yes, you in?' At the time, I was feral and stupid enough to agree, so off we went.

When we arrived at the nearby Iraqi town, the local people swarmed our ambulance. They knew we were there to help because of the big red cross displayed on our converted Humvee ambulance. We proceeded to triage and administer medical care to those who needed it most.

After forty-five minutes or so, out of the corner of my eye, I saw a blue Nissan truck racing toward us with two Iraqi men in the cab. Adrenaline coursed through my veins and anxiety shot through my body. I yelled out to Rezek, 'Hey man we have trouble coming.'

We both made ready our 9mm Berettas and mentally prepared for the worst. But as the two men approached, we saw the look on their faces, and we could tell they were actually in need of help and not a threat. As the truck slowed to a stop, the passenger side door swung open and an elderly man signaled us for help. He introduced himself as Muhammad and then lifted his leg out of the cab of the truck, exposing an infected wound on his lower leg. He was in bad shape; he had lost a bunch of weight, was febrile, and looked like death.

We started an IV line and administered antibiotics. We removed the dead skin surrounding the wound, bandaged him up, and gave him oral antibiotics to take for the next few weeks. And what happened next is something I will never forget. It has become my greatest memory and lesson from my time in the military, one that still teaches and inspires me today.

When we were through treating him, the old man stepped out of his truck to thank us. His eyes began to well up with tears; I can only imagine he was shocked by the way we cared for him. I will never forget the way he looked at us, shook our hands, and then hugged Rezek and I. For some reason, in that moment, my life was marked by Muhammad's gratitude. I will never forget that day for as long as I live.

Throughout our lives, we will have the great opportunity to move outside of ourselves and help others. When we act on these opportunities, we create a space in time to be rewarded, to be marked forever, by the gratitude of others.

People we have yet to meet desperately need us, and we were made—not for ourselves—but for others. The experiences we gain by helping others are invaluable and powerful. I hope this encourages you to find a way to use your unique gifts to serve others in some small way.

This brilliant quote by N. Eldon Tanner gets to the heart of the matter:

> *"Service to others is the rent we pay*
> *for the privilege of living on earth."*

Creativity

"Imagination is more important than knowledge." Albert Einstein

Have you drawn, painted, built, sculpted, colored, or written something in the last few months? When was the last time you created? Some may not be able to recall the last time they created something, but what if I would have asked you the same question when you were five years old? Surely, your answer would have been, yes.

But as time relentlessly marches on, seemingly taking us hostage along with it, many of us deactivate our creative minds, and set them aside. We trade them in for the logic-based utilitarian minds, the ones that get us through the workday. Invariably, after some time goes by without creating, we forget about our powerful ability to bring unique ideas into existence through our creative force. Kevin Kelly understands the power of creativity and shares:

> "Anything real begins with the fiction of what could be. Imagination is therefore the most potent force in the universe, and a skill you can get better at. It's the one skill in life that benefits from ignoring what everyone else knows."[34]

All of us were born with the innate capability to dream something up and bring it into existence. The *homo sapiens* is the most elaborate creation and most capable creator on earth. Our ability to think abstractly and create from an abstract power source is one of the few things that separates us from the animal kingdom. However, somewhere along the journey of 'growing up,' many have reasoned themselves into an all or nothing, black or white, type of thinking, and have concluded they are either creative or not.

Many believe that creativity only exists in some special subset of humans, a minority population that is congregating late at night in theatres and art galleries, when in fact—we are all capable of creating.

A revealing study was conducted by George Land. He tested the creative ability of 1600 students, at the age of five years old, then again at ten years old, and at fifteen years old. At five years old, 98 percent of the students scored highly creative, genius level, for creativity. At ten, the same set of students were tested, and only 30 percent scored as highly creative. Again, the same students were tested at fifteen years old, but only 12 percent scored as highly creative. Land was intrigued by the results, and so the test was then given to 280,000 adults who were over twenty-five years old, and the percentage of highly creative individuals was recorded at a staggering 2 percent.[35]

Why do we lose our creativity over time? Could it be that our creativity leaks out or wanes away from us somehow on our journey to adulthood? Maybe. But it is more likely that we conform to societal pressures and norms of thinking; we are slowly but surely poured into the mold of a 'typical worker,' the final product resembling what our economies and education systems demand.

At an early age we begin learning formulas, principles, habits, methods, and best practices. We are taught what to do and especially what not to do; therefore, it is likely we transmute into the humdrum, the mechanized world, the rank and file, eventually becoming learned out of our creativity.

Howard Thurman urged, "Don't ask what the world needs. Ask what makes you come alive, and go do it. Because what the world needs is people who have come alive."

Einstein may have said it best when he stated, "Imagination is more important than knowledge." But why did one of the most capable thinkers and scientists of the modern world place imagination at a level higher than knowledge? It is likely Einstein understood knowledge is merely a collection of facts, beliefs, and principles—that before knowledge or any data can become useful, imagination and action must be applied to them. Could it have been Einstein knew the power of creativity and its implications for the creator and society?

Mihaly Csikszentmihalyi, a psychologist, author, and distinguished professor, has studied happiness and focus for decades; through his research, he has discovered and named a psychological concept called flow, a highly focused mental state conducive to productivity. His findings state that creativity is, "a central source of meaning in our lives … most of the things that are interesting, important, and human are the results of creativity … when we are involved in it, we feel that we are living more fully than during the rest of life."[36]

Could it be that when creators bring things to life, works of art, new inventions, alternative business models, they too come alive?

Creators change the world by inventing alternatives to the past, new sources of options in a society. Creators enable others to dream in vivid detail, escape from the mundane by introducing them to new forms of entertainment, paintings to admire, and symphonies that transport the mind into a state of wonder.

Think of the last movie you watched—one that captivated your imagination and will stay with you for some time. For me, it was the movie *1917*. The film grabbed me by the senses and strapped me into a creative roller coaster. I had the feeling I was traveling alongside Lance Corporal Schofield, dodging rounds, traversing barbed wire, and being starved of food. I was a partner in his hero's journey, and while the trials were almost insurmountable, together we made it.

Creators have power to transport the minds and emotions of others, to take them on an excursion without ever knowing them. They have the magical ability to rescue one from the pressures of life and carry them safely to Never Never Land, Sherwood Forest, or Pandora, the world James Cameron created in *Avatar*, where global audiences met and fell in love with the sagacious Na'vi species.

The power to impress and transport the thoughts and emotions of others is not only done through motion pictures. It has been done over the decades through writing and other mediums. Consider Homer's *Odyssey*, written in the eighth century BC. It still captures the imagination of readers today. Or, consider the great creator Michelangelo who painted the ceiling of the Sistine Chapel in the early sixteenth century. For over four hundred years it has drawn curious onlookers from around the world to gaze at its beauty.

Cameron, Homer, and Michelangelo all have something in common with every other human throughout history and present day, and that is—everyone has a story to tell, a story that is unique to them. One of the greatest human desires is to be known, to be heard out, to share their story with others. The great creators have chosen to express themselves through story or some other form of enchantment, and so can you.

The importance of creativity finally settled in for me when I heard Fredrik Härén say, "We are most like God when we are creating."

The reality of the quote is unknown, but its implications, if true, are limitless for creators. Every individual has a unique story to tell, a contribution to share, a masterpiece in life to create.

Be encouraged to share and practice your creativity with others. You and your creations may be the spark that ignite another's soul. Share your creativity through a short story, a doodle, direct it in a movie, or paint it on a chapel ceiling. You were born with the ability to create, so could it be—you were meant to be seen, be heard, begin creating?

Adventure

*"To dare is to lose one's footing
momentarily. Not to dare is to lose
oneself." Soren Kierkegaard*

Adventure does something to the soul. It pries open the eyelids of the slumbering mundane and shocks the heart into a state of vivid consciousness. There is something magical about chasing a dream, living out an adventure, or risking it all. When we adventure, we burn the ships and make the decision there is no way but forward. When we add *venture* to our lives, we forge into the unknown territory that the scared masses eye in fear.

It is a bold endeavor to live adventurously. When most of society sets the example of seeking safety and finding comfortable routine, something inside of the bold adventurer says, 'I won't have it.' Great nations were built by the adventurous few, not the safe masses. Inventions and discoveries that changed world history were accomplished by one decision—to set course for the adventure of a lifetime.

Why is it that each of us is born as an individual, but over the course of some time, becomes homogeneous? Slowly but surely, we are trained to look and think and act a certain way, when everything inside of us says, 'break free.' Adventure calls out to the unique. It says, 'come and be you.' It says, 'you were born unique with purpose for a time like this.'

Adventure does not have a certain look. To be adventurous does not mean one must set sail and discover a new land like Columbus did. An adventure starts with one step into the unknown, one pivot in a different direction from the masses, and one degree of movement, even if only a micro-shift, toward individualism. We must dare to adventure if we want to come alive.

What adventure have you kept lying dormant in the basement of your heart? When we repress our adventurous nature, it fades and is eventually absorbed by normalcy. So, pull out your stops, and take up the adventure of your lifetime. There is no time like the present, and waiting for the perfect time is always an excuse born from fear. A fear of what 'might happen' is a faceless excuse that must be discarded if we want to live a life of adventure.

At age twenty-one I found myself in the middle of the Iraq War. One day I was hit with the reality that I may never get a chance to see Baghdad, the capital of Iraq and epicenter of the war. I decided to ask one of my buddies to cover my Marines since I was their first line of medical care. After he agreed, I snuck onto another Marine unit's five–ton troop carrier headed to Baghdad.

It was an adventure into the center of chaos. It was risky, but I needed to come alive more than I needed to feel comfortable. Later that day, I returned and was greeted by a pissed off Marine captain, our company commander, who called me into his command tent and demanded to know where I had been. The commander screamed at me while his face turned various shades of red, told me I was irresponsible for not clearing the trip with him first, and then threatened to ruin me, whatever that meant, to keep me from future trips of similar nature.

Was the adventure worth the risk? Absolutely! It was reckless abandon and selfish of me, but when I reflect on that day, the experience helped me break through a very morbid time and feel alive. When we take a risk and venture into the unknown, we are always rewarded by the experience, and if nothing else, we rid ourselves of regret and the stifling effects of fear.

At the end of our life, we will survey our choices, time on Earth, and the risks we took. We will look back and conclude either, 'fear held us back,' or 'we lived an adventure.' How will you answer your call to adventure?

> *"Life is either a daring adventure or nothing at all." Helen Keller*

Conclusion

What do we do with all of this information? To paraphrase Peter Drucker, all of the knowledge in the world is just meaningless data until we apply action to it.

My hope is that you set this little book nearby, maybe on your nightstand or desk, so when life hits you with something, a challenge or a doubtful season, you can turn back to a section of the book that will encourage you.

This is all my best; I hope and pray that it speaks to you and serves you well.

Your friend, Terry Weaver

Quote Index

A Dream

"The tragedy of life is what dies inside a man while he lives." Albert Schweitzer

"Never give up on a dream just because of the time it will take to accomplish it. The time will pass anyway." Earl Nightingale

Fear

"The price of our vitality is the sum of all our fears." David Whyte

"Life expands and contracts in proportion to one's courage." Anaïs Nin

Hope

"What lies behind us and what lies before us are tiny matters, compared to what lies within us." Ralph Waldo Emerson

"To live as if we are dying gives us a chance to experience some real presence. Time is so full for people who are dying in a conscious way ...." Anne Lamott

Criticism

"You don't always have to chop with the sword of truth. You can point with it, too." Anne Lamott

Challenges

"Obstacles are those frightful things you see when you take your eyes off the goal." Henry Ford

Work

"My experience has been that work is almost the best way to pull oneself out of the depths." Eleanor Roosevelt.

"I don't know what your destiny will be, but one thing I do know. The only ones among you who will be really happy are those who have sought and found how to serve." Albert Schweitzer

The Herd

"Heaven knows, punishment and trance are a great deal more comfortable and familiar than aliveness." Anne Lamott

Desperation

"The mass of men lead lives of quiet desperation." Henry David Thoreau

"Be yourself, everyone else is taken." Thomas Merton

"The only thing we have to fear is fear itself." Franklin D. Roosevelt

Genius

"Whatever you can do, or dream you can do, begin it. Boldness has genius, power, and magic in it." William H. Murray

Anger

"Anger is often what pain looks like when it shows itself in public." Krista Tippett

"Where a man's wound is, that is where his genius will be." Robert Bly

Words

"The effect you have on others is the most valuable currency there is."
Jim Carrey

Forgiveness

"If you wish to travel far and fast, travel light. Take off all your envies, jealousies, unforgiveness, selfishness, and fears." Glenn Clark

"Forgiveness is a gift you give yourself." Maya Angelou

Good and Evil

"The line separating good and evil passes ... right through every human heart" Aleksandr Solzhenitsyn

Gardening

"The revelation of thought takes men out of servitude into freedom."
Ralph Waldo Emerson

Love

*"Love is always a risk, it's daring;
without courage, it's impossible"
Terry Weaver*

Seeking

*"What you seek is seeking you."
Rumi*

*"When you die you take absolutely
nothing with you except your
reputation." Kevin Kelly*

Perfection

*"It's more important to know where
you are going than to get there
quickly. Do not mistake activity for
achievement." Isocrates*

Mental Maps

*"Life can only be understood
backwards; but it must be lived
forward." Soren Kierkegaard*

Worship

*"A person will worship something ...
Therefore, it behooves us to be
careful what we worship, for what we
are worshipping, we are becoming."
Ralph Waldo Emerson*

Identity

*"The privilege of a lifetime is being
who you are." Joseph Campbell*

*"Life isn't about finding yourself, it's
about creating yourself." Unknown*

*"The thing that is really hard, and
really amazing, is giving up on being
perfect and beginning the work of
becoming yourself." Anna Quindlen*

The Mind

*"Life is a process of becoming, a
combination of states we have to go
through. Where people fail is that
they wish to elect a state and remain
in it. This is a kind of death."
Anaïs Nin*

"The best defense is a good offense."
Historical Military Tactic

Strategy

"Strategy without tactics is the slowest route to victory. Tactics without strategy is the noise before defeat." Sun Tzu

Fundamentalism

"A fundamentalist is a person who considers whether a fact is acceptable to his religion before he explores it." Seth Godin

"The revelation of thought takes men out of servitude into freedom."
Ralph Waldo Emerson

"The very reason I write is so that I might not sleepwalk through my entire life." Zadie Smith

Influence

"When all is said and done, more will be said than done." Aesop

More

"If I wanted to destroy a nation, I would give it too much, and I would have it on its knees, miserable, greedy, sick." John Steinbeck

"The care of $200 million is enough to kill anyone. There is no pleasure in it." W.H. Vanderbilt

"I was happier when doing a mechanic's job." Henry Ford

"I have made many millions, but they have brought me no happiness." John D. Rockefeller

"Millionaires seldom smile." Andrew Carnegie

Busyness

"Beware the barrenness of a busy life." Socrates

Focus

"Simplicity is the ultimate sophistication." Socrates

"I can't give you a surefire formula for success, but I can give you a formula for failure: try to please everybody all the time." Herbert Bayard Swope

"An investment in knowledge pays the best interest." Benjamin Franklin

Connection

"You know the problem with the rat race is, even if you win, you're still a rat." Lily Tomlin

Time Travel

"The whole future lies in uncertainty: live immediately." Seneca

"This only is denied, even to God: the power to undo the past." Agathon

Company

"The unexamined life is not worth living."
Socrates

"People do not seem to realize that their opinion of the world is also a confession of character." Ralph Waldo Emerson

"Sometimes it takes darkness and the sweet confinement of your aloneness to learn anything or anyone that does not bring you alive is too small for you." David Whyte

Communication

"When there is a lack of communication, people go negative."
Jon Gordon

"That which is most personal, is most general." Stephen Covey

Superpower

"If you speak when angry, you'll make the best speech you'll ever regret." Groucho Marx

Wisdom

"Every man I meet is my superior in some way. In that, I learn of him."
Ralph Waldo Emerson

"When the student is ready, the teacher will appear." Ancient Proverb

Responsibility

"The price of greatness is responsibility." Winston Churchill

"Don't ever take a fence down until you know the reason it was put up."
G.K. Chesterton

"The greatest good you can do for another is not just to share your riches but to reveal to him his own."
Benjamin Disraeli

Service

"Service to others is the rent we pay for the privilege of living on earth."
N. Eldon Tanner

Creativity

"Imagination is more important than knowledge." Albert Einstein

"Don't ask what the world needs. Ask what makes you come alive, and go do it. Because what the world needs is people who have come alive." Howard Thurman

"We are most like God when we are creating." Fredrik Härén

Adventure

"To dare is to lose one's footing momentarily. Not to dare is to lose oneself." Soren Kierkegaard

"Life is either a daring adventure or nothing at all." Helen Keller

References

Hope
1) Lamott, Anne. *Bird by Bird: Some instructions on Writing and Life*. New York: Doubleday, 1994.

Criticism
2) Roosevelt, Theodore. *Citizenship in a Republic.* A lecture delivered April 23, 1910. Paris, France.

3) Pressfield, Steven. *The War of Art: Winning the Inner Creative Battle*. New York: Black Irish Entertainment LLC, 2002.

Challenges
4) Isaacson, Walter. *LEONARDO DA VINCI*. New York: Simon & Schuster, 2017.

Desperation
5) Thoreau, Henry David. *Walden and Other Writings of Henry David Thoreau*. Edited by Brooks Atkinson. New York: The Modern Library, 1992.

Genius

6) Lexico Powered by Oxford. Genius definition. https://www.lexico.com/en/definition/genius

7) Moore, Robert and Gillette, Douglas. *King Warrior Magician Lover: Rediscovering the Archetypes of the Mature Masculine*. New York: HarperOne, 1990.

8) McChrystal, Stanley, Eggers, Jeff and Mangone, Jason. *Leaders: Myth and Reality*. New York: Penguin Random House LLC, 2018.

9) Wikipedia, Ludwig Van Beethoven. https://en.wikipedia.org/wiki/Ludwig_van_Beethoven#Family_and_early_life

10) Jordan, Michael. Speech delivered on September 11, 2009. Naismith Basketball Hall of Fame

11) Murray, William Hutchison. *The Scottish Himalayan Expedition*. United Kingdom: Dent, 1951.

12) 1 Peter 4:10

Words

13) Carrey, Jim. Commencement speech delivered at Maharishi International University class of 2014. https://www.youtube.com/watch?v=V80-gPkpH6M

14) Proverbs 18:21

Good and Evil

15) Solzhenitsyn, Aleksandr. *Gulag Archipelago*. New York, Harper & Row, 1985.

Seeking
   16) Proverbs 4:7-9

Mental Maps
   17) Serani, Deborah Psy.D. *Two If It Bleeds, It Leads: Understanding Fear-Based Media.* Psychology Today posted June 7, 2011. https://www.psychologytoday.com/us/blog/two-takes-depression/201106/if-it-bleeds-it-leads-understanding-fear-based-media

Worship
   18) Merriam-Webster. Definition of Worship https://www.merriam-webster.com/dictionary/worship
   19) Nasaw, David. *Andrew Carnegie.* New York: Penguin Group, 2006.
   20) Burge, Gary M. and Green, Gene L. *The New Testament in Antiquity, 2nd Edition: A Survey of the New Testament within Its Cultural Contexts.* Grand Rapids: Zondervan Academic, 2020.
   21) Wikipedia. Westminster Shorter Catechism. https://en.wikipedia.org/wiki/Westminster_Shorter_Catechism

Strategy
   22) Fables of Aesop. Fablesofaesop.com https://fablesofaesop.com/the-lion-in-love.html
   23) Wikipedia. Trojan Horse. https://en.wikipedia.org/wiki/Trojan_Horse

Fundamentalism

24) Open Culture. Openculture.com posted November 16, 2016. http://www.openculture.com/2016/11/the-new-york-times-first-profile-of-hilter.html

25) Wikipedia. Time Person of the Year. https://en.wikipedia.org/wiki/Time_Person_of_the_Year

More

26) Alcorn, Randy. *Money, Possessions, and Eternity*. Carol Stream, Il: Tyndale House Publishers, Inc., 2003.

Focus

27) Pressfield, Steven. *The War of Art: Winning the Inner Creative Battle*. New York: Black Irish Entertainment LLC, 2002.

28) Microsoft Attention Span Study, 2015. https://terryweaverbooks.com/wp-content/uploads/2020/04/Microsoft-Attention-Spans-Research-Report.pdf

29) Newport, Cal. *Deep Work: Rules for Focused Success in a Distracted World*. New York: Grand Central Publishing, 2016.

Communication

30) Gordon, John and Smith, Mike. *YOU WIN IN THE LOCKER ROOM FIRST: The 7 C's to Build a Winning Team in Business, Sports, and Life*. Hoboken NJ: John Wiley & Sons, Inc., 2015.

Superpower

31) Frankl, Viktor E. *A Man's Search for Meaning.* Boston, MA: Beacon Press, 2006.
32) Proverbs 17:28

Responsibility

33) Frankl, Viktor E. *A Man's Search for Meaning.* Boston, MA: Beacon Press, 2006.

Creativity

34) Kelly, Kevin. kk.org. Posted April 28, 2020. https://kk.org/thetechnium/68-bits-of-unsolicited-advice/
35) Land, George and Jarman, Beth. *Breakpoint and Beyond: Mastering the Future Today.* New York: HarperCollins Publishers, 1992.
36) Csikszentmihalyi, Mihaly. *Flow: The Psychology of Optimal Experience.* New York: HarperCollins, 1990.

About the Author

In 1999, Terry Weaver enlisted as a U.S. Navy corpsman. He was deployed as a combat medic with the U.S. Marines and served in Kuwait and Iraq from 2002 to 2003. After five years of active duty, Terry received an honorable discharge.

He attended Mays Business School at Texas A&M and received the Pat Tillman Foundation Scholarship established in the namesake of Army Ranger and NFL star player, Pat Tillman, who was killed in action. Terry earned a Bachelor of Business Administration.

In 2019, Terry wrote and published *The Evolution of A Leader*, and in 2020 he wrote and published *A Dark Day in Texas*, a fiction novel.

Terry is happily married to Chelley Weaver, who has encouraged him to chase his dreams and walk in faith. Terry has four beautiful children: Laura, Zen, Presley and Liam. Terry and his family reside in Houston, Texas. Connect with Terry on Facebook at www.facebook.com/terryweaverbooks/

Made in USA - North Chelmsford, MA
1174838_9781733090247
10.06.2020 0946